IN AN ISLAMIC STATE

MALIK SAIF-UR-RAḤMĀN

2015

ISLAM INTERNATIONAL PUBLICATIONS LIMITED

Minorities in an Islamic State
By Malik Saif-ur-Raḥmān

First Published in *The Review of Religions* Rabwah
September, October 1963 & February, March 1974

Present Edition in UK in 2015

Published by:
Islam International Publications Ltd
Islamabad
Sheephatch Lane
Tilford, Surrey
United Kingdom GU10 2AQ

Printed in UK at:
Raqeem Press
Islamabad
Tilford, Surrey, GU10 2AQ

ISBN: 978-1-84880-849-2

Foreword to the Present Edition

Minorities in an Islamic State, the book in your hand, is the English translation of the book, *Islam aur Ghair Muslim Ri'āyā,* by the late Malik Saif-ur-Raḥmān Sahib. This translation was published in *The Review of Religions* Rabwah September, October 1963 & February, March 1974, without the name of the translator. We have tried, but have not so far been successful, to find out who the translator was. I hope we shall be able to mention his name in the next edition.

Now we are publishing it as a booklet according to the instructions of Ḥaḍart Mirzā Masroor Aḥmad Khalīfatul-Masīḥ V (May Allah be His Helper) for the benefit of a wider readership.

I hope that this timely publication would go a long way to rebutting the criticism of the West against Islam—at least as far as the aspect of it dealt with herein is concerned—and to changing their views about it, and demolishing the self-contradictory concept of the 'militant Islam'.

It needs to be acknowledged, with gratitude, that with the help of Central Research Cell, Rabwah, we have updated and corrected all the references in the works cited herein.

I am grateful to Mirzā Anas Aḥmad, M.A. M. Litt. (Oxen), Wakīlul-Ishā'at for checking and correcting the script where necessary.

Munir-ud-Din Shams
Additional Wakīlut-Taṣnīf London
July 25, 2015

Publishers' Note

The name of Muhammad, the Holy Prophet[sa] of Islam, has been followed by the symbol [sa], which is an abbreviation for the salutation *Ṣallallāhu 'Alaihi Wasallam* (may peace and blessings of Allah be upon him). The names of other Prophets and Messengers are followed by the symbol [as], an abbreviation for *'Alaihis-Salām* (on whom be peace). The actual salutations have not generally been set out in full, but they should nevertheless, be understood as being repeated in full in each case. The symbol [ra] is used with the name of the companions of the Holy Prophet[sa] and those of the Promised Messiah[as]. It stands for *Raḍiyallāhu 'anhu/'anha/'anhum* (may Allah be pleased with him/with her/with them). [rh] stands for *Raḥimahullāhu Ta'ālā* (may Allah have mercy on him). [at] stands for *Ayyadahullāhu Ta'ālā* (may Allah be his Helper).

In transliterating Arabic words we have followed the following system adopted by the Royal Asiatic Society.

ا — at the beginning of a word, pronounced as *a*, *i*, *u* preceded by a very slight aspiration, like *h* in the English word 'honour'.

ث — *th*, pronounced like th in the English word 'thing'.

ح — *ḥ*, a guttural aspirate, stronger than h.

خ — *kh*, pronounced like the Scotch ch in 'loch'.

ذ — *dh*, pronounced like the English th in 'that'.

ص ṣ, strongly articulated s.

ض ḍ, similar to the English th in 'this'.

ط ṭ, strongly articulated palatal t.

ظ ẓ, strongly articulated z.

ع ‘, a strong guttural, the pronunciation of which must be learnt by the ear.

غ *gh*, a sound approached very nearly in the r '*grasseye*' in French, and in the German r. It requires the muscles of the throat to be in the 'gargling' position whilst pronouncing it.

ق *q*, a deep guttural k sound.

ء ’, a sort of catch in the voice.

Short vowels are represented by:

a for ـــَـــ (like *u* in 'bud');

i for ـــِـــ (like *i* in 'bid');

u for ـــُـــ (like *oo* in 'wood');

Long vowels by:

ā for —ا— or آ (like *a* in 'father');

ī for ی —ِ— or —ٖ— (like *ee* in 'deep');

ū for و —ُ— (like *oo* in 'root');

Other:

ai for ی —َ— (like *i* in 'site')♦;

au for و —َ— (resembling *ou* in 'sound').

Please note that in transliterated words the letter 'e' is to be pronounced as in 'prey' which rhymes with 'day'; however the pronunciation is flat without the element of English diphthong. If in Urdu and Persian words 'e' is lengthened a bit more it is transliterated as 'ei' to be pronounced as 'ei' in 'feign' without the element of diphthong thus 'کے' is transliterated as 'Kei'. For the nasal sound of 'n' we have used the symbol 'ń'. Thus Urdu word 'میں' is transliterated as 'meiń'.*

The consonants not included in the above list have the same phonetic value as in the principal languages of Europe.

We have not transliterated Arabic words which have become part of English language, e.g., Islam, Mahdi,

---

♦ In Arabic words like شیخ (Shaikh) there is an element of diphthong which is missing when the word is pronounced in Urdu.

* These transliterations are not included in the system of transliteration by Royal Asiatic Society. [Publishers]

Quran**, Hijra, Ramadan, Hadith, ulema, umma, sunna, kafir, pukka etc.

For quotes straight commas (straight quotes) are used to differentiate them from the curved commas used in the system of transliteration, ‘ for ع, ’ for ء. Commas as punctuation marks are used according to the normal usage. Similarly for apostrophe normal usage is followed.

The Publishers

** Concise Oxford Dictionary records Quran in three forms—Quran, Qur’an and Koran. [Publishers]

بِسۡمِ اللّٰہِ الرَّحۡمٰنِ الرَّحِیۡمِ[i]

The Meccans and the Advent of the Prophet[sa]:

The claim of the Holy Prophet[sa] as a divinely inspired Reformer angered the people of Mecca. The Chiefs of Quraish decided to oppose Islam. The idol-worshippers would not tolerate the new religion to spread in Arabia. They were determined to crush Islam in the very beginning. They decided to employ all means at their disposal to deal with this menace. The common folk joined the Quraish in their fight against the Muslims. There started a period of severe trials and hardships for the Muslims. Their lives, properties and honour were in constant danger. They were beaten, boycotted and abused. They were denied even the ordinary civic rights that every citizen enjoyed. It was impossible for them to preach their religion or even to praise it openly. To accept Islam, even to praise it openly, at that time meant death. Even the Prophet[sa] was no exception to this. He was insulted and abused. To give but one example of the way in which the Meccans treated him, we reproduce here a tradition by Ḥaḍrat 'Ā'ishah[ra] — wife of the Prophet[sa]. She reports that referring to these days of troubles and miseries the Holy Prophet[sa] once said:

---

[i] In the name of Allah, the Gracious, the Merciful. [Publishers]

> "Abū Lahab and 'Utbah were my neighbours. I was hemmed in on all sides by their schemes and machinations. To make life difficult for me they would deposit the heaps of night soil at my door steps. I would remove this dirt when I came out and would only say, 'O sons of 'Abd-e-Munāf, why all this? Is this the way you discharge your neighbourly duties"?[1]

As is clear from the above Hadith the Quraish spared nothing to prevent people from accepting Islam. They were determined to put an end to the new religion which was gaining converts from among their co-religionists. One can easily feel the intensity with which the inhabitants of Mecca hated the innocent Muslims and their pious leader. This insulting behaviour of the Meccans towards Muslims and the ugly manner in which they treated them, forced the Muslims to leave Mecca and seek refuge somewhere else.

The Result of Persecution:

The Muslims went to Yathreb—a town some 200 miles north of Mecca—where the Prophet[sa] had some followers. But even their migration did not appease the anger of the Meccans. Instead, they became all the more bitter and violent in their opposition. They would not let the Muslims live in peace and safety.

They planned to pursue the fugitives to Medina and to slaughter them. Many a time with large armies equipped with powerful weapons did they attack the Muslims. The Muslims met the invaders bravely and resisted their advances. Keeping in view the small number of the followers of the Prophet[sa], as compared to the Meccans, their phenomenal victory over their opponents cannot be explained except that this miracle was brought about solely through the grace of God.

These wars were fought in pure self-defence. It was only in their self-defence that the Holy Prophet[sa] ordered the Muslims to take up arms. No one can show that the Holy Prophet[sa] ever fought with the Meccans or, for that matter, with any other enemy except to defend himself. Even his critics admit that he fought because he was compelled to fight.

As the Muslims were never the first to attack their enemies but made war in order to save their own lives, they were helped and aided by the Almighty God and it was through His help that they were able to return as victors, to the city from which they had been driven out by force.

Prophet's[sa] Greatness:

One can judge from the following illustration the Prophet's[sa] tenderness of heart and the love that he felt for his fellow human beings. In the hour of his triumph, when he had the power to avenge himself over his persecutors, he forgave them all.

It is reported that

> "before his migration to Medina, the Holy Prophet[sa] once asked ‘Uthmān bin Ṭalḥah—the keeper of the keys of Ka‘bah—to open the door of the House of Allah. Most arrogantly he refused to comply with the request. At this, the Holy Prophet[sa] said, 'A day will come when these keys would pass into my hands and I will give these keys to whomsoever I would like'. With great contempt and derision, ‘Uthmān exclaimed 'Will the sons of Quraish be powerless on that day!' On the day of the Fall of Mecca, the Holy Prophet[sa] went to Ka‘bah and summoned ‘Uthmān in his presence. Trembling he came and stood before the Holy Prophet[sa] cowering in fear and remembering how he had once treated the Prophet[sa]. Disregarding his unseemly behaviour the Holy Prophet[sa] forgave him and addressed him in tones full of love and kindness, 'You are pardoned, ‘Uthmān, because today is the day of forgiveness and not of revenge. You are also appointed the keeper of Ka‘bah’s keys and whosoever tries to take away these keys from you shall be treated as a usurper".[2]

Such was the conqueror of Mecca! On that day he had the right and the power to avenge injuries done to him. The proud Meccans were at his mercy. He could have done whatever he wished. But he forgave them all! The gentleness with which he treated his violent enemies won for him a large number of converts from among his early opponents. Yet there remained certain tribes who, in spite of becoming his subjects, preferred to remain faithful to their old religion.

The Institution of *Dhimmiyyat*:

Now when we try to find out a reasonable excuse for the Meccans to justify their unseemly behaviour towards the Holy Prophet[sa] and his followers, we have to admit failure. For the Holy Prophet[sa] was a peaceful and peace-loving citizen. Even before the Call, he was known for his deeds of charity and selfless service. He was called *Amīn*[i] and *Ṣādiq*[ii] by those who later became his most bitter enemies. He was famous for his honesty, integrity and moral uprightness, for his participation in the affairs of social and national importance. He called the people to worship One God, to give up their evil ways and to shape their lives according to the highest moral and

---

[i] The one who can be fully trusted. The Holy Quran says رَسُوْلٌ اَمِيْنٌ i.e. Messenger faithful to his trust. (26:108)
[ii] Truthfull

ethical standards. He advised them to help the needy and the poor.

In all this there was nothing that could have aroused their anger. But in spite of the peaceful attitude of the Prophet[sa] towards them and the reasonableness of his teachings, the Meccans would not let him live in peace. They tried to stop Muslims from practicing Islam freely by the use of brute force. The Muslims were denied the fundamental human right namely the freedom to profess and practice their faith. Now with the coming of Muslims in power, the non-Muslims were naturally anxious for their future under the new regime. They were anxious because they knew that the war between them and the Muslims was fought on the question of religious freedom. They knew that in their days of power they had denied this right to the Muslims and now they were afraid that living under a Muslim government they might not be allowed to practice their faith. The point was the same, only the balance of power had shifted in favour of the Muslims. But the Holy Prophet[sa] told the non-Muslims that although he had won the victory yet he would uphold the principle for which he fought with them. He declared that the Muslims would feel it obligatory upon them to protect the right of freedom of religion of every individual. He told them that they would be *Dhimmīs* of the Muslims and that Allah and his Prophet would be responsible to safeguard their interests. He granted to the non-Muslims all the rights that the Muslims enjoyed. Their lives, properties and honour were made as sacred and inviolable as those of the Muslims.[3]

Dhamma is an Arabic word from which the word *Dhimmī* is derived, which means one who is granted every kind of protection and safety.

It is clear from what has been said above that according to the Islamic law the Muslims and the non-Muslims stand on an equal footing in matters of fundamental human rights. No distinction was ever made between the rights of Muslims and non-Muslims. This Charter of freedom granted by the Holy Prophet[sa] was well expressed by Ḥaḍrat 'Alī[ra] when he said:

> "*Dhimmīs* have agreed to pay *Jizyah* for the reason that their lives may be treated as the lives of Muslims and their properties as the properties of the Muslims. Therefore, in these matters, there is no distinction between the rights of the Muslims and *Dhimmīs*".[4]

Again we see that the pact concluded between Ḥaḍrat 'Umar[ra] and inhabitants of Jurjān ran thus.

> "The lives, properties, communal life, identity and the religion of the population of Jurjān shall

be safeguarded. No change shall be brought about in their status nor shall they be interfered with in any way".[5]

Equality between the Muslims and the non-Muslims:

We have seen the provisions of the Charter of freedom defining the rights of the *Dhimmīs,* or non-Muslims, permanently granted to them by the Holy Prophet[sa]. Let us, now, examine the rights that the Muslims enjoyed in order to determine if the non-Muslims were really given a fair deal under Islam. Referring to the fighting tribes, who were erstwhile enemies of the Muslims, the Holy Prophet[sa] said:

"I have been commanded to fight those who have violated the sacred right of religious freedom and have destroyed my right to live peacefully. But those who accept God as One, worship Him the way we do, adopt our *Qiblah*[i] as their own and do not object to eating meat as prepared by us or in other words agree to become Muslims and give up fighting against us—all their former misdeeds shall be forgiven. Since Allah and His Prophet have taken upon themselves the duty of protecting them, it is

[i] The Ka'bah diversion or the direction to which Muslims face when saying their prayres.

incumbent on Muslims who hold the reigns of power to discharge this duty zealously and never underestimate its importance".[6]

This positive statement of the Holy Prophet[sa] clearly shows that he gave exactly the same rights to *Dhimmī* non-Muslims as were given to the combatant tribes who accepted Islam.

It is on the basis of this equality of the rights that Muslim jurists have defined the rights of non-Muslim citizens in a Muslim State, in the following words:

> "If the non-Muslims chose to live under a Muslim State and agree to pay its taxes, they will enjoy the same rights and privileges as are enjoyed by Muslims at large. Similarly they will be asked to discharge same obligations as the Muslims are required to discharge."[7]

Dhimmīs—an Honourable Title:

In short, it was this declaration of protection of and responsibility for the non-Muslims, on the basis of which the non-Muslim citizens of a Muslim state were described as *Dhimmīs*. True, this term has come to carry some dangerous connotations because of its wrong interpretation by some ignorant Mullahs. But in the great days of early Islam, the term *Dhimmī* signified the sacred responsibility of Muslims to protect all the rights of the non-Muslim citizens, and that the non-Muslims would have the fullest opportunities to live in peace without the least threat or danger to their security. The term *Dhimmīs* was a source of pride both for the Muslims and non-Muslims.

The institution of *Dhimmīs* contained the secret of the greatness of a government; and the public, irrespective of creed or community to which it belonged, took pride in being the citizens of a state of this kind. The term, at no stage, signified restraint against the fundamental rights of an individual nor did it mean to subject him to the restrictions of a subject and a slave.

That in the days of the Holy Prophet[sa] and his successors, this principle of equality was followed in its highest sense is an open chapter of World history. No distinction was made between a Muslim and a non-Muslim in social and civic affairs. Every officer of state was issued clear directions particularly to protect the rights of non-Muslim citizens, to respect their dignity and honour and not to give them any cause or occasion for complaint.

The Holy Prophet's[sa] Sociological Relations with the Non-Muslims:

The Holy Prophet[sa] as the head of the Islamic state treated the non-Muslims on a footing of absolute equality and tried successfully to establish good business and social relations with them.

Thus we see that once he borrowed some money from a Jew. After some time the Jew came to realize his loan, he was rather rude and insulting in his behaviour towards the Holy Prophet[sa]. He used such language that the companions of the Holy Prophet[sa] flew into rage. But the Prophet[sa] restrained them and said:

> "Please let him alone. He has the right to say what he has said because I owe him what he demands".[8]

After this the Prophet[sa] paid him the money he owed. Eventually the Jew accepted Islam when he experienced such good treatment at the hands of the Prophet[sa].

Once a Jewess who was a *Dhimmiyah* from Khaiber tried to poison him by offering him some poisoned roasted meat. On being found out she apologized and instead of punishing the Prophet[sa] forgave her.[9]

Anas[ra] reports that the Prophet[sa] accepted the invitation of a Jew and willingly partook of the humble fare of fat and oat meal.[10]

Ibn-e-Abī Lailā relates that one day Suhail bin Ḥanīf and Qais bin Sa‘d were sitting in Qādsiyyah, when a funeral procession passed by, the two got up to respect the dead. Somebody pointed out that the funeral was that of a non-Muslim; whereat the two replied:

> "What does it matter, do you not remember that when once a funeral procession passed by the Holy Prophet[sa], he got up. The people pointed out that it was the funeral of a Jew. The Prophet[sa] replied, 'Do you not think the Jews too are human beings'."[11]

Abū Hurrairah[ra] reports that once a non-Muslim stranger stayed with the Prophet[sa] as a guest. The Prophet[sa] milked one of his goats and offered the milk to the guest. But the guest was not satisfied. The Prophet[sa] offered him the milk of a second goat, but the guest was still not satisfied. In fact he drank the milk of as many as seven goats. The Prophet[sa] was amused at his hunger but would say nothing.[12]

Moreover the Holy Prophet[sa], as a matter of habit, used to visit the ailing non-Muslims to express sympathy with them and to share their sorrows and sufferings.[13]

Protection of the Rights of *Dhimmīs*:

Bilāl[ra], who handled the domestic expenses of the Holy Prophet[sa], borrowed some money from a *Dhimmī*, for use in the Prophet's[sa] house. The day on which the loan was to be repaid was approaching fast but there was no money. Bilāl[ra] was afraid that the creditor would press his demand and make things awkward for him. He conveyed his fears to the Prophet[sa] and begged leave to go out of Medina for a few days to escape from the clutches of the creditor. Under the law of the time a money-lender could even put the borrower under house arrest. Bilāl[ra] was afraid that this too might happen. Accordingly, he went to his house and made preparations to go out of the city early in the morning. Early next morning, Bilāl[ra] received word from the Prophet[sa] that he need not worry as arrangements for payment had been made.[14]

This happened sometime after seventh year of Hijra when Islam was at the heyday of its power. World history is incapable of furnishing a similar example of the protection of rights of an ordinary citizen against the head of a state.

Soon after the Fall of Mecca, a deputation of Banū Thaqīf from Ṭā'if waited on the Holy Prophet[sa], who made arrangements for their stay in the Mosque, where tents were pitched for them. Some people approached the Prophet[sa] and objected to their staying in the mosque on the ground that the guests were idolaters and an impure lot. The Prophet[sa] replied that the Quranic verse إِنَّمَا الْمُشْرِكُونَ نَجَسٌ i.e. "The idolaters are impure" refers to a condition of heart and not to that of the body. Nor for that matter is any human being impure in this sense. Bodily speaking all human beings are pure and have the right to free access to the holiest of holy places.[15]

Muḥayyiṣah[ra], one of the companions of the Prophet[sa], was killed in Khaiber. His heirs filed a suit for blood money before the Holy Prophet[sa]. The Holy Prophet[sa] asked them if they could swear to the identity of the murderer. They replied:

> "O Prophet[sa] of Allah, we did not happen to be present at the time of murder, how can we testify on oath".

The Prophet[sa] replied:

> "You cannot claim damages without proof. The only alternative that remains under the law is that the Jews of Khaiber whom you suspect, should fifty times plead not guilty to the charge to clear their position."

The heirs of the late companion said:

> "The Jews are not reliable, they can easily make false statements and swear to their truth".

The Holy Prophet[sa] declared:

> "Then I can't do more than this, because the Quranic law does not allow any discrimination".

It is interesting to note that the Prophet[sa] paid the damages to the heirs of Muḥayyiṣah[ra] out of his own pocket.[16]

Once some Muslims, who were fed up with the machinations of the Jews of Khaiber, misappropriated some of their fruits and animals. The Prophet[sa] was furious when he came to learn of this and said:

> "Allah does not allow you to enter the houses of the People of the Book without their permission. Similarly it is absolutely illegal to pluck fruits from their orchards".[17]

An Anṣārī reports:

> "Once I accompanied the Prophet[sa] on a journey. I was hungry and had nothing to eat. I spotted some goats belonging to some non-Muslims, which I captured, killed and put the cauldron on fire. Meanwhile the Holy Prophet[sa] arrived and came to know of what I had done. He had a bow in his hand, with which he struck at the cauldron and threw it away, and declared, 'loot is as illegal as a dead carrion'."[18]

It is reported in the *Musnad Imām Aḥmad bin Ḥanbal* that once some children were overtaken by the rush of battle and were trampled to death. The Prophet[sa] was shocked at this, to console him one of the companions submitted:

"O Prophet[sa] of Allah, after all they were only children of the idolaters".

The Prophet[sa] said:

"The Children of idolaters are also humans like you, and have the inherent capacities to become the best of men. As a matter of fact every child is born a Muslim, it is after his birth that his parents make him a Jew, a Christian or something else. Beware! do not kill children. Beware! do not kill children."[19]

Justice by Muslims:

'Abdullāh bin Rawāḥah[ra] was appointed collector of Khaiber by the Holy Prophet[sa]. The Jews of Khaiber entered into an agreement with the state to pay half the annual yield of land as tax. When the harvest would be ready he would offer the Jews the option to divide it into two equal shares and give him the first choice, or let him divide the harvest into two shares if they wanted the first choice. At this just offer the Jews were touched and exclaimed.

"God is our witness, that it is justice of this kind on which the equilibrium of the earth and the heavens rests". [20]

Once a Muslim and a Jew had a quarrel and came to 'Umar[ra], the second Khalīfah, for adjudication.

After hearing the two parties and finding the Jew was in the right he decided in his favour. At this the Jew exclaimed:

"By God! You have judged rightly".[21]

Islamic history is full of examples of a similar kind. The judiciary was absolutely independent and the judges used to give their verdict without any fear or favour. Even the head of the state could be summoned to the court and satisfy the demands of justice as an ordinary citizen. Little wonder therefore if the non-Muslim prospered under the Muslim rule and were immune from inroads against their fundamental rights, conscience, life and property.

Treatment of *Dhimmīs* by the Muslims:

Before the advent of Islam, the Persian and the Roman empires exercised great influence over the Arabian Peninsula. With the establishment of a strong Muslim government of the Country their influence was bound to decrease. Fearing this, they decided to attack the Muslims and began preparations for the invasion. In these circumstances the Muslims were compelled to take up arms to defend themselves against aggression and advanced against the territories held by the Persians and the Romans.

Those were the dark days of religious and ideological persecution. The poor people of these areas were treated by the Emperors and their officers in an unthinkably cruel and ugly manner. The Jews, the Christians and the man in the street were subjected to all sorts of cruelties by the Persian monarchs. They were robbed of their properties and honour. Protests were quelled by death, torture and extortion. The same was the case with the subjects of the Caesar. The Unorthodox there, were similarly victimized. The lower classes were being bled to death. It was an all round atmosphere of repression. Under the circumstances the freedom of belief, the freedom of conscience and the tolerance shown by the Muslims was bound to create, in the minds of these people, a sense of relief and freedom.

How much these poor people were overwhelmed by the kind treatment of Muslims can be seen by an incident that took place in Ḥimṣ.

Once, under pressure of the Roman army, the Muslims had to retire from Ḥimṣ. The Muslims had already collected taxes from the inhabitants of the territory. Before leaving the place, they returned all the taxes which they had realized and declared:

> "These taxes were realized on the condition that we would be responsible for your security and for the maintenance of law and order in this area. As we are forced to leave this place, we are no

longer in a position to fulfil this condition."

History has recorded the reply of the people of Ḥimṣ in the following glorious words:

> "We were the victims of cruelty and repression at the hands of our co-religionists. Then you people came. Your justice and the way you governed us had won our hearts. Now we will fight shoulder to shoulder with you against the armies of Hercules and he can advance only over our dead bodies".

The Jews went so far as to swear in the name of Torah that they will not let the enemy enter the city. Thus the whole of the population of the area rose against the Romans with the consequence that they were forced to retreat. On their victorious return in the city, the Muslims were accorded a rousing reception by the citizens. They took out processions and sang and danced to express their joy on the triumphant return of the Muslims. [22]

Again we see that when Ḥaḍrat 'Umar[ra], the second caliph, passed from Adhri'āt on his way to Jerusalem, the Christian inhabitants of the area welcomed him by the blowing of bugles and the beating of drums and by showering flowers on him.

Ḥaḍrat 'Umar[ra] took great care in respecting the sentiments of the Christians and the Jews. Once he enquired of a Christian deputation, if the Muslim officers of their province behaved properly and were just. They replied:

> "We have seen nothing of Muslims except good treatment and morals".

The buildings of the Government house and the treasury in Kūfah were designed and built by a famous non-Muslim architect named Rozbah. The governor of Kūfah was pleased at his performance and sent him to Ḥaḍrat 'Umar[ra] in Medina. Ḥaḍrat 'Umar[ra] received him graciously and ordered that he should be given a generous annuity for the rest of his life.[23]

Islam's concern about the protection of the rights of minorities can be judged by the fact that the wills of the Prophet[sa], of Abū Bakr[ra] and of 'Umar[ra] contained the following injunction.

> "Be good to the *Dhimmīs*, be generous and tolerant towards them, and do not let them come to any harm".[24]

The Basic Necessities of *Dhimmīs*—a Government Responsibility:

The agreements concluded between the Muslims and the non-Muslim inhabitants of the conquered territories always contained the provision that the Muslim government would be responsible for the basic necessities of the *Dhimmī* citizens. This, for instance, is an extract from the agreement with the citizens of Ḥīrah:

> "The *Dhimmī* who is old or is disabled in some accident or is otherwise unable to work or one who is rich but falls destitute, he and his dependents, will not only be exempted from all taxes, but will also be paid subsistence allowance from the government treasury".[25]

Similarly it was laid down that if a *Dhimmī* fell into the hands of an enemy and his release depended on ransom, the money would be paid by the Muslim government.[26]

History bears out how this principle was followed by the Muslim governments. To quote only one instance:

Ḥaḍrat 'Umar[ra] once came across an aged *Dhimmī* in rather a sad plight. On seeing the poor condition of the old *Dhimmī*, Ḥaḍrat 'Umar[ra] exclaimed:

> "By God! It is not just that in his youth we may benefit from his youth and leave him to suffer in his old age".

He ordered that the old *Dhimmī* be given a pension till his death. Moreover he directed the governors that the poor and deserving among the

Dhimmīs, in their provinces, be regularly paid stipends from the *Baitul-Māl*.[27]

Non-Muslim's Participation in Administration:

Ḥaḍrat 'Umar[ra] always used to consult *Dhimmīs* in the affairs of state. When the question of land settlement in Iraq arose, he called a meeting in Medina to decide the matter. In this meeting the non-Muslim Chiefs of Iran and Iraq also participated.[28]

Again we see that in settling the affairs of Egypt, Ḥaḍrat 'Umar[ra] always consulted Maquqas—the religious leader of the Egyptians before taking any decision.[29]

Similarly a Nestorian priest, a contemporary of 'Umar[ra], writing about the political conditions of his area, says in a letter to a friend of his:

> "The Muslims protect our religion, respect our priests and Pharisees and have bestowed lands and Jāgīrs on our churches".[30]

It is also worth noting that the Muslim caliphs used to invest the religious leaders of the *Dhimmīs* with certain civil and administrative powers.[31]

The Muslims continued to treat the non-Muslims throughout the centuries in a similar manner. The door of every office of the government was open to them and they were given a fair deal in these matters. Thus we see that under the Umayyads and Abbassides, the

Dhimmīs were not only always consulted by the rulers but they were also appointed to the highest civil and military offices under the caliph. Thus, Ḥaḍrat Amīr Mu'āwiyah's personal physician and court interpreter, Ibn-e-Āthāl, who was a Christian, was appointed the governor of Ḥimṣ by the Amīr.

Even as late as the days of Aurangzeb in India it is recorded that once a Muslim officer of state objected to the appointment of two non-Muslim in his department on the basis of the Quranic verse:

يٰۤاَيُّهَا الَّذِيْنَ اٰمَنُوْا لَا تَتَّخِذُوْا عَدُوِّيْ وَعَدُوَّكُمْ اَوْلِيَآءَ

> "O ye who believe! take not My enemy and your enemy for friends".(60:1)

On this application the Emperor remarked:

> "Noted the contents of your application. Let it be clear once and for all that no Parsi or Hindu government servant can be dismissed simply because he is a non-Muslim. The verse that you have quoted in your report does not at all prove that a Muslim should have no relationship whatsoever to a non-Muslim. In fact, you have not quoted the verse in full, the complete verse is as follows:

يٰٓاَيُّهَا الَّذِيۡنَ اٰمَنُوۡا لَا تَتَّخِذُوۡا عَدُوِّىۡ وَ عَدُوَّكُمۡ اَوۡلِيَآءَ تُلۡقُوۡنَ
اِلَيۡهِمۡ بِالۡمَوَدَّةِ وَ قَدۡ كَفَرُوۡا بِمَا جَآءَكُمۡ مِّنَ الۡحَقِّ ۚ يُخۡرِجُوۡنَ
الرَّسُوۡلَ وَ اِيَّاكُمۡ اَنۡ تُؤۡمِنُوۡا بِاللّٰهِ رَبِّكُمۡ ؕ

"O ye who believe! take not My enemy and your enemy for friends, offering them love, while they disbelieve in the truth which has come to you *and* drive out the Messenger and yourselves *from your homes merely* because you believe in Allah, your Lord'. (60:1)

"This shows that this verse prohibits the Muslims to have relations only with those non-Muslims who compelled the Holy Prophet[sa] to migrate from his city by inflicting all kinds of cruelties on him and with those who did their most to persecute the Muslims. But there are others who are not like them and God does not forbid the Muslims to maintain good relations with, and to be generous to, them. Thus in another verse in the same chapter as the one quoted above God says:

لَا يَنۡهٰىكُمُ اللّٰهُ عَنِ الَّذِيۡنَ لَمۡ يُقَاتِلُوۡكُمۡ فِى الدِّيۡنِ وَ لَمۡ يُخۡرِجُوۡكُمۡ
مِّنۡ دِيَارِكُمۡ اَنۡ تَبَرُّوۡهُمۡ وَ تُقۡسِطُوۡۤا اِلَيۡهِمۡ ؕ اِنَّ اللّٰهَ يُحِبُّ
الۡمُقۡسِطِيۡنَ ۝

"Allah forbids you not, respecting those who

have not fought against you on account of *your* religion, and who have not driven you from your homes, that you be kind to them and act equitably towards them; surely Allah loves those who are equitable.(60:9)

"Therefore if your interpretation of the verse quoted by you were true, it would have been obligatory upon us to kill all the Rājās and non-Muslim subjects of India. The fact, however, is that the verse absolutely does not mean what you say. The offices of state are open to all, on the basis of ability and competence, irrespective of caste or creed. As far as religion is concerned, we should follow the Divine word: لَكُمْ دِينُكُمْ وَلِيَ دِينِ. i.e. 'For you your religion and for me mine'." (109:7)[32]

Equality Before Law:

The status of Muslims and *Dhimmīs* was equal in the eyes of law. No distinction was ever made between a *Dhimmī* citizen or a Muslim in a judicial inquiry. No one can show a single instance of favouring a Muslim against a *Dhimmī*. They were treated alike and were given equal opportunities to defend themselves in case of a trial. It is a matter of record that a Muslim guilty of any offence against a *Dhimmī* never went unpunished. In short we see that the example of the Holy Prophet[sa] and his pious

Successors shows clearly that under the law, civil and criminal, all are equal and must be treated alike, irrespective of their religious or social status.

Once during the days of the Holy Prophet[sa], a Muslim murdered a *Dhimmī*. The case was brought before the Holy Prophet[sa] for trial. The Holy Prophet[sa] decided that the Muslim being guilty of murdering another human being must be put to death. He further declared:

أَنَا أَحَقُّ مَنْ أَوْفَى بِذِمَّتِهِ

> "To protect the rights of *Dhimmīs* is my most important duty".[33]

Similarly, once a Muslim who had murdered a *Dhimmī*, was brought before Ḥaḍrat 'Alī[ra]. It was found that the accused was guilty. Accordingly, 'Alī sentenced him to death. The relations of the culprit persuaded the heirs of the victim to pardon the crime on payment of blood money. When Ḥaḍrat 'Alī[ra] came to know of this he sent for the brother of the deceased and said:

> "Perhaps these people have tried to secure your consent under duress".

He replied:

> "No I did it out of my own free will without any pressure. As putting the murderer to death

> cannot bring my brother back to life, the blood money they are giving me, will, to some extent, sustain the survivors and therefore, I have decided to pardon him".

Ḥaḍrat 'Alī[ra] replied:

> "It is all right if you really mean it, you know better. However, the policy of our government most emphatically is, that the blood of a *Dhimmī* citizen is as valuable as our own blood and his blood money is equal to ours".[34]

Once a son of 'Amar bin al-'Āṣ, the governor of Egypt, gave a beating to a *Dhimmī* citizen without any justification. The incident was reported to Ḥaḍrat 'Umar[ra]. Under his orders the governor's son was publicly beaten by the Egyptian *Dhimmī*. 'Umar[ra] also declared in his order to the governor:

مُنْذُكَمْ تَعَبَّدْتُّمُ النَّاسَ وَقَدْ وَلَدَتْهُمْ أُمَّهَاتُهُمْ اَحْرَارًا

> "Since when have you taken people as slaves although they are born free."[35]

The occasion on which the Quranic verse: وَلَا تَكُنْ لِّلْخَآئِنِيْنَ خَصِيْمًا "And be not thou a disputer for the faithless" (4:106) was revealed is the following:

Once a Muslim stole something from someone's house. Fearing exposure, he threw away the stolen property in a Jew's house, which was recovered on investigation. The Jew pleaded not guilty, but the culprit insisted that the Jew was the thief. Some other people seem to have supported the Muslim on the available evidence and denounced the Jew as being guilty. The Holy Prophet[sa], too, thought, may be the Jew was responsible for the theft. It was on this occasion that God revealed the above given verse and informed the Prophet[sa] of the true facts. The Muslim was accordingly punished because of the theft and for misstatement. The Holy Prophet[sa], further, forbade the Muslim from quarrelling with the Jew.[36]

Jizyah:

Jizyah was a tax realized from the non-Muslim citizens of a Muslim state. The one condition basic to its realization was that it was to be imposed only on those males who were able to earn and did actually earn. Those below 20 and above 50, as also women, the insane, the slaves, the disabled, the paralytic, the deaf, destitute, monks and priests, and the members of fighting forces were exempt from this tax. Even a rich man could claim relief from this tax in case of a year's long unemployment.[37]

Three different categories of assesse males were defined to determine their financial status. Normal rate of *Jizyah* was three rupees per annum. It was six rupees yearly from the middle class people and 12 rupees from the rich. Almost the whole of the tax so realized was spent on the education, development, uplift and welfare of the *Dhimmīs*.[38]

Actually, in those days, the Muslims were under conscription and under the law had to do compulsory military service. The *Dhimmī* citizens, however, were under no such obligation and were given the option, either to enlist in the army like the Muslims or to pay a token tax, on payment of which they were guaranteed protection and security against external as well as internal aggression. Therefore it was that those who paid the tax were automatically exempted from service in the army. Thus one clause of the pact signed at the time of the fall of Jurjān is as follows:

> "We agree to guarantee protection and security to you on the condition that you continue to pay tax, which will be remitted in case you choose to join the army or civil service".[39]

Jizyah—Not a Religious Tax:

It must be pointed out that *Jizyah* was not a religious tax. Even before the Muslims this tax was there and people used to pay it. As a matter of fact, there is historical evidence to prove that the tax under the Muslims was exactly the same as the tax levied by Nosherwan's government in Iran. The famous Christian historian Jurjy Zaidan writes thus:

"In the 5th century B.C. *Jizyah* was imposed on the inhabitants of Asia Minor by the Greeks who took them under protection and saved them from the attacks of Phoenicians. These people used to pay it gladly enough in lieu of the security of life they enjoyed under the Greeks. Similarly they imposed an annual tax of 9 to 15 guineas on the residents of France when they conquered Gaul. From Greeks the tax was adopted by the Persians who called it Gazeet, which means, money the government realizes from the citizens every year. *Jizyah* is the Arabic form of Gazeet. Hence it was not a religious tax by any means and was in fact an age old tax, on payment of which the government guaranteed the security of citizens."[40]

On the other hand the Muslims were not exempt from taxes. They had to serve in the army in lieu of *Jizyah* and apart from voluntary contributions and emergency collections they had to pay an annual tax called *Zakat* which was calculated on the basis of the value of their total holdings. The Muslim citizens, therefore, were under a much greater burden, for, in addition to service in the army, they had to pay more than *Dhimmī* citizens.

Charters of Human Equality:

In the 4th year of Hijra, the Holy Prophet[sa] gave a signed guarantee of protection to the monks, priests and Christians of St. Catherine's Church near Mount Sinai. In this guarantee the Prophet[sa] laid down:

> "It is the duty of Muslims to safeguard the Christian churches, monasteries and their holy places against trespass by the enemy and to protect the Christians fully from all harm and injury. They should not be unduly taxed, nor should they be forced to quit. No Christian should be compelled to forsake his religion. No Monk should be expelled from his monastery, nor should any pilgrim be stopped from visiting any holy place. No Christian church should be razed to the ground or occupied to provide accommodation for Muslims or their mosques.
>
> "It is the duty of the Muslims to give unqualified and unconditional help to the Christians in the construction of their churches and shrines, and in any other religious matter in which they need help".

Then addressing the Muslims, the Prophet[sa] said:

> "Do not think that by doing the things mentioned in the guarantee, you participate in promoting their religion, because the real intent of this order is to remove any difficulty which they feel,

> and submission to these orders is in reality the submission to the orders of the Prophet of God which he has issued under Divine Command".

He further advised the Muslims:

> "Even in time of war, in fact when the Muslims are actually engaged in fighting against the Christians, do not harbour feelings of hatred and enmity against a Christian who lives among you. If any Muslim shows such behaviour towards a Christian, he will be considered an aggressor and a rebel".

The Holy Prophet[sa] further declared:

> "If any Muslim is guilty of violating any of the above given orders, he will be denounced as one who has broken the Divine Covenant, has violated His express injunctions and who has humiliated and shamed the religion of Islam".

Quoting this guarantee, a famous European historian and orientalist declares it to be a great Charter of 'Human Equality and Freedom' and a 'document of Human brotherhood which establishes the greatness of the guarantor'.[41]

The Sermon which the Prophet[sa] gave at the time of the Last Pilgrimage to Mecca is a Masterpiece of Human Equality and Brotherhood, he said:

"O Men! Your Maker is One; you are the sons

> and daughters of one father, therefore no attempt at dividing you into high and low is acceptable; No Arab has any superiority to a non-Arab nor has a non-Arab any superiority to an Arab; neither the Whites are superior to the Blacks nor are the Blacks superior to the Whites. The only mark of excellence is the fear of God and an individual's personal virtue and piety. Under an Islamic State race and colour have no distinction".

Continuing the Prophet[sa] said:

> "As you respect this day; this month and this land of pilgrimage, so shall you respect the life, property and honour of every human being, which, under the law, are as sacred and inviolable".[42]

It is not surprising that after such a declaration of human equality and brotherhood the Muslims were welcomed with open arms wherever they went and conquered more than half of the known world in a span of a few years. Needless to say that it was not a triumph of superior Muslim arms, but a victory of a superior law which appealed to the heart and won it.

It is a pity that this golden rule did not last long. The Khilāfat gave way to monarchy and the rights of the Muslims became insecure and the sanctity of their lives and property was violated by the authorities, and many of their eminent leaders and theologians suffered torture and injustice. Naturally the rights of the *Dhimmī* citizens were also jeopardised. Almost the same situation arose which was ostensibly the case of the downfall of the Roman and Persian empires. It must, however, be pointed out that breach of trust and mischief on the part of *Dhimmīs* were in no small measure responsible for this change. Because, the passage of time made them ungrateful and they had forgotten the way the Muslims had rescued them from the tyrannies of their co-religionists. Because of this they had started transferring their loyalties to the non-Muslim states. This changed political situation affected the thinking of jurists and commentators of law. They framed rules and regulations about *Dhimmīs* which had no sanction of Sharī'ah. It is not very pleasant to discuss these laws in detail, but, unfortunately, we have to, in order to present a complete picture of the circumstances prevailing at the time. Our duty, therefore, is twofold: First, what are the injunctions of Islam about the non-Muslim citizens of a Muslim state, and secondly, to define the misconceptions about these injunctions which were caused directly by political reasons.

An amazing prophecy about the downfall of Muslims:

First of all it would not be out of place to discuss a prophecy of the Holy Prophet[sa] of Islam. In this prophecy there are certain pointers to the political downfall of Muslims which had a close bearing on the subject under discussion. The prophecy is as follows. Once Ḥaḍrat Abū Hurairah[ra] addressing a party of Muslims, said: "Your plight would be sad indeed when your government would face serious financial and economic crises and you will not be able to realize anything from *Dhimmīs* on a voluntary basis." Some of the amazed listeners asked, if things would really come to such a pass? Abū Hurairah[ra] replied: "God is my witness, that the Holy Prophet[sa] told me, 'When the trust of God and the Prophet[sa] shall not be honoured and the *Dhimmīs* shall not be respected, their hearts in their turn will become hardened and they will refuse to pay *Jizyah*'."[43]

It is a pity that in spite of this the Muslims failed to heed this timely warning. The question, how and why this happened, will be answered in the light of the rules laid down by the jurists which are reproduced below.

The so-called Juridical Rules about the *Dhimmīs*:

The first restriction which the jurists were inclined to impose because of a number of reasons was to establish a visible mark of distinction between the Muslim and non-Muslim citizens.

(1) The mentality which led to the application of this distinction demanded that these signs of distinction should be derogatory to the *Dhimmīs* so as to make them appear inferior to the Muslims. The author of *Hidāyah*, discussing the necessity of establishing such a distinction writes:

> "The *Dhimmīs* should be forced not to imitate the Muslims in dress, and not to have similar mount nor to saddle them. They should, in fact, be better advised to be different from the Muslims in their use."[44]

Next follow the details of this distinction. For example, "The dress of the *Dhimmīs* should be of a coarse quality; it should not be silken or of other costly fibre. Their shirts should not be low; shoes should be ugly and ill-shaped and should be made of something rough and coarse, they should have a finger-thick, woollen waistband of prescribed specification. This waistband was formally known as *Kastīj* which is an ancient Persian word and means, humiliation and insult. That is why this band could not be of silk because silk adds to gracefulness, and therefore defeats the very purpose, which is to disgrace and humiliate *Dhimmīs*; otherwise, too, it produces in the poorer Muslims a sense of inferiority. Also the *Dhimmīs* must not wear robes which the Muslims wear. They should also not be allowed to wear the dress of the learned and the scholar.[45]

(2) The second distinction pertains to the mounts that the *Dhimmīs* should possess. It was laid down that they could, however, ride a mule or a donkey. Even then they could not use saddle meant for horse, instead they should use only an inferior kind of saddle meant for pack animals. Some jurists have gone to the length of insisting that the *Dhimmīs* should not use any animals as mounts. They permit its use only in cases of extreme emergency, for instance, when a patient is to be removed or when the journey is very long. But even then they are required to dismount and walk on foot when they pass a Muslim colony".[46]

(3) The third article lays down that the *Dhimmīs* should affix prescribed signs on their houses as marks of distinction so that everybody should know that they belong to *Dhimmīs*. This would save Muslims from inadvertently praying for their forgiveness. Again, their houses should in no way be higher than the houses of Muslims. Muslim women should observe purdah from the *Dhimmī* women as they do

from the men. If any *Dhimmī* woman tries to see a Muslim woman, she should be punished. The paths and baths for Muslim and *Dhimmī* women should be kept separate, so that there is no intermixing among them. The *Dhimmīs* should not be greeted first. They should be told not to walk in the middle of the roads. A *Dhimmī* should not be allowed to sit if a Muslim is standing. If he keeps on sitting he should be regarded disrespectful and arrogant. The Muslims should never show any respect for the *Dhimmīs*.[47]

(4) It was proposed that the *Dhimmīs* could not erect their places of worship and cemeteries in *Dārul-Islam*. Old buildings could however, be renovated but without any structural addition. The *Dhimmīs* are not allowed to build new places of worship because according to traditions Islam does not permit it. *Dārul-Islam* means a town or a village where congregational prayers of Jumu'ah and 'Īd are offered; and arrangements exist for the execution of sentences. According to some, Muslim towns are of three kinds: (a) Those founded by the Muslims themselves for instances; Baṣrah, Kūfah, Baghdad, Wasat, etc. Non-Muslims will not be allowed to build their houses of worship in such cities. Nor will they be allowed to carry out their religious activities in open. (b) The cities which the Muslims conquered. Here, too, the *Dhimmīs* are not allowed to build their

temples. (c) Cities acquired peacefully through treaties. Here the authorities should act as the terms of agreement demand. They are, however, advised that they should try not to agree to a treaty that gives this right to the *Dhimmīs*. In case this right is given, they should try to avoid its implementation. In their religious festivals, too, the *Dhimmīs* are not allowed to take out procession of their idols, images or crosses outside their temple nor are they allowed to stage any religious demonstration in public. It is also not advisable for Muslims to attend non-Muslim temples, not because they haven't the right but because such places are the houses of the devils and only the devils assemble there.[48]

(5) Every *Dhimmī* should pay *Jizyah* personally. He is not allowed to do so through any representative or advocate. The *Jizyah* paying *Dhimmī* must stand when he pays while the Muslim collector should keep sitting, and he should hold the *Dhimmī* from his collar and give a good shake saying: "pay up! you enemy of God".[49]

The alleged utility of Juridical stipulations about *Dhimmīs*:

It is interesting to note that the Jurists who framed these anti-*Dhimmī* rules have offered justifications for these rules which are simply amazing. For instance, according to these jurists, such restrictions are necessary in order to expose the *Dhimmīs* to humiliation and emphasize their impotence. This would protect the weak Muslims. Also, according to them, the *Dhimmīs* must be disgraced, as much as the Muslims have to be honoured. Therefore it is, that if there is no mark of distinction between the Muslim and Non-Muslims, there is every possibility that a *Dhimmī* might be confused with a Muslim and honoured and respected like him which according to them is dangerously illegal. Hence the necessity of such distinctions. But care should be taken to see that these restrictions and marks lower rather than enhance the self-respect of *Dhimmīs*. Because political expediency demands that these people are kept weak and suppressed.[50]

Some apologists have tried to justify the imposition of such restrictions on the ground that it was meant to promote the interest of the *Dhimmīs* themselves. It was actually, they say, a protective measure for the safeguard of their culture and civilization. Such marks of distinction, for example, would help the Muslims recognize the *Dhimmīs* more readily and this according to them held the hands of the ordinary Muslims and obviated the chances of clash against the *Dhimmīs*. It is clear that justifications of this trend can satisfy only those modern imperialists of East and West who try to prove that their colonial strongholds in Asia and Africa are meant purely to serve the People of these countries, to confer on them the blessings of learning and knowledge, to civilize them and ultimately to enable them to take over the reins of power.

Some people try to save face by saying that such oppressive measures were proposed by irresponsible and unauthentic people or that they have been handed down to us by not very reliable quarters. To us, this answer, too, holds no water, because the details reproduced above have been taken from standard works of Islamic jurisprudence. For instance, *Hidāyah* is one of the most famous books of *Fiqah*[i] and one of the basic ones, too. It is part of recognized syllabus on *Fiqah* and accepted by almost all the centers of Islamic learning throughout the Islamic world. Its commentary فتح القدير (*Fatḥul-Qadīr*) was written by no less an expert on Islamic law than Abū Hammām. Similarly بحر الدقائق (*Baḥrud-Daqā'iq*) a commentary of كنز الدقائق (*Kanzud-Daqā'iq*) is a standard work, بداء الضاء (*Badā'uḍ-Ḍā'*) is also an authoritative work of Hanifite school of *Fiqah*. 'Ainī's commentary of كنز الدقائق (*Kanzud-Daqā'iq*) and Fatāwā Sharā'i are equally authoritative works.

[i] Islamic jurisprudence.

And who can doubt the authenticity of Imam Novi's commentary of Saḥīḥ Muslim. Similarly الاختيارات العلميه (*Al-Ikhtiyārātul-'Ilmiyyah*) has been compiled by the famous Imam Ibn-e-Taimiyyah. In short, all works that have been quoted above are standard and authentic. In their day all these books have been important sources of governmental policy.

It must not, however, be misunderstood that the views expressed by these authors have Islamic sanction at their back. We merely want to point out that these details in fact exist in books on Islamic jurisprudence. Again it should be clearly understood that these rules were not always followed by the Muslim governments. As a matter of fact in spite of these ridiculous sanctions, Muslims and their governments generally, were very generous towards the *Dhimmī* citizens in keeping with the true spirit of Islam. This had been admitted by the non-Muslims themselves. The famous Christian historian Jurjy Zaidan who is well-known for his hostility against Muslims, writes:

> "One of the important causes of the rapid scientific advancement by the Muslims was that Muslim caliphs encouraged and honoured scholars and scientists irrespective of their nationality and religion. They were famous for bestowing huge rewards and honours on them.

Differences of religion, nationality and race were not even thought of Christians, Jew, Sabians, Sumarians, Majosites, all were equally favoured and respected by the caliphs. The non-Muslims enjoyed the same rights to freedom and status as did the Muslim nobles and high officials."[51]

Again when the repeated violation of treaties and border trespasses by the Roman Qaiser's armies had taxed caliph Haroon's patience to its limits, one day he angrily demanded the chief justice Imam Abū Yūsuf as to why in spite of all these violations the Christians remained safe under the Muslims and who allowed them to take out open processions of Cross in the cities. At this Imam Abū Yūsuf with great courage and calmness replied: "When these countries were conquered in the days of Ḥaḍrat 'Umar[ra], (the second Khalīfah of the Holy Prophet[sa]) it was guaranteed to the Christians that their churches will remain inviolate and that they shall have full freedom to religious observances and take out processions of cross openly. Therefore no one has the right to cancel this order which relates to basic human rights".[52]

Similarly writing about the Muslim rule in Spain the author of the History of Spain, Louis Bertrand, says:

"The Christians were left masters of it. They retained their estates, together with timber,

> dwellings, and all movable property; and they retained also, the right of sale."[53]

These facts bear out that even after the days of the pious Caliphate the Muslim governments' attitude towards their non-Muslim citizens, to say the least, was full of affection and regard and was based on the principles of equality and Justice. They, in fact, paid scant respect to these legalistic innovations of jurists. It is not, however, denied that when a corrupt ruler was guilty of trespass against the rights of *Dhimmī* citizens, in order to fulfil his ulterior designs, he tried to justify his excesses by basing them on such juridical monstrosities, and gave excesses by basing them on such juridical monstrosities, and gave the non-Muslim critics an opportunity to criticize Islam.

Are these restrictions based on any clear Islamic Injunctions?

Let us at this stage try to find out what after all, if any, is the ultimate sanction under Islamic law which could justify these restrictions. Does the Holy Quran deal with these restrictions? Or can they be traced back to Sunna and the practice of the Holy Prophet[sa]? The answer to these questions had better be given in the words of these jurists themselves.

> "If the right to impose these restrictions against the *Dhimmīs* is challenged on the ground that in the days of the Holy Prophet[sa] such restrictions

were conspicuous by their absence, and they are not, therefore, permitted under the Sharī'ah, the answer is that in the days of the Prophet[sa] the number of *Dhimmīs* was very small indeed and they were known to all. The question of mistaking their identity, therefore, could not arise. But in the days of Ḥaḍrat 'Umar[ra], the need arose to impose such restrictions. He even ordered imposition of such restrictions in the presence of a large number of the companions of the Holy Prophet[sa], none of whom objected to this step of Ḥaḍrat 'Umar[ra].[54]

In the foregoing passage the jurists themselves confess that in the august days of the Holy Prophet[sa] such restrictions against the *Dhimmīs* did not exist. They also admit that under Ḥaḍrat Abū Bakr[ra] too, these restrictions were non-existent. As for as Ḥaḍrat 'Umar's[ra] Khilāfat is concerned, historical evidence conclusively proves that his days, too, are free from the blot of such restrictions and give a lie to the claims of the jurists, which is supported neither by internal nor external evidence. The so-called treaty on which the jurists rely and which has been reported by Ibn-e-Mandah runs as follows:

"The Christians of Syria and this town sign this instrument of surrender to be submitted to the servant of Allah the commander of the faithful,

'Umar. Your armies overpowered us in the battlefield. We, therefore, seek protection under you for ourselves and for our families, for our properties and for our nation. In return, we undertake to abide by the following conditions which we have voluntarily offered out of our own free choice. In our cities or their suburbs, we will build no new church or monastery, nor shall we rebuild the old churches. Similarly, we will not stop Muslims who come from outside from staying in the churches, day or night, their doors shall remain open for them. We shall also consider it our duty to extend to them our hospitality for three days. We shall not permit spies against the Muslims to take refuge in the churches. We shall not permit our children to study the Holy Quran. We shall neither preach nor practice *shirk* or *Bid'at*. Nor shall we stop the people from accepting Islam. We shall esteem the Muslims for whom we shall stand up and make room when we receive them in our midst. We shall not imitate the dress the Muslims wear and shall not follow their hairstyle. We shall not speak the Arabic language. Nor shall we permit the use of family names like the Muslims. We shall ride bare-back. We shall not engrave Arabic letters on our sings. We shall not trade in liquors in the Muslim habitations. We shall shave the hairs on the frontal of our heads as a mark of distinction. We shall wear Zunnar round our waists. We shall not take out processions of the cross or the holy books in Muslim areas, or shall we display the cross or the images, nor ring church-bells before the Muslims".[55]

In point of *sanad*[i] this treaty is most suspect. غرائب الشعبه (*Gharā'ibush-Shu'bah*) is not at all an authoritative book on Hadith, nor does it have any historical importance whatsoever. What is more, this treaty reported by Ibn-e-Mandah is in flagrant conflict with the Instrument of Protection which the Holy Prophet[sa] granted to the monks of St. Catherine's monastery and which has already been quoted above. To say that Ḥaḍrat 'Umar[ra] did something which was diametrically opposed to what the Holy Prophet[sa] did or that he was even ignorant of the existence of this instrument of protection is, to say the least, historically false. Further, the confused style and the ill-assorted internal structure of the so-called treaty are enough to establish that it is a mere myth and fabrication. Throughout the Muslim history, never has any restriction been placed on the study of the Holy

[i] Chain of narrators of Hadith.

Quran by the non-Muslims. Instead the Holy Quran repeatedly invites the non-Muslims to consider and ponder its message. Says the Holy Quran:

اَفَلَا يَتَدَبَّرُوْنَ الْقُرْاٰنَ

"Will they not, then, ponder over the Quran". (47:25)

Elsewhere it says:

وَلَقَدْ يَسَّرْنَا الْقُرْاٰنَ لِلذِّكْرِ فَهَلْ مِنْ مُّدَّكِرٍ ۝

"And indeed we have made the Quran easy *to understand and* to remember. But is there anyone who would receive admonition?" (54:18)

How could a book with this message support any restriction on its study. Similarly no embargo has ever been placed on the study of Arabic language. There have been a host of non-Muslim scholars of Arabic language. It is an historical fact that when Ḥaḍrat 'Umar[ra] visited Jābiyah in Syria, the man who interpreted his addresses to the people there was a Christian priest who was a deputy to the Bishop and occupied a high office in the church.[56] Similarly who can deny the poetic excellence of اخطل (Akhtal) who was a famous Christian poet in the court of Umayyad Caliphs. The personal physician and his official interpreter Ibn-e-Assal was also a Christian.

What is more important is that the Muslims have always respected and preserved the sanctity of non-Muslim temples. They have never allowed any Muslim to violate their sanctity by staying in them. On the other hand the Muslims themselves have inserted this condition in many of the agreements they signed that they would not let any Muslim reside in non-Muslim temples. For instance, this condition is very much clear in their agreement with the Christians of Jerusalem. It is interesting to note that this agreement was signed by Ḥaḍrat 'Umar[ra] himself. We reproduce parts of the treaty in support of our thesis:

> "This is the pledge of protection granted by the Servant of Allah, Commander of the faithful, 'Umar, to the people of Elia. This protection covers their lives and properties, their sick and healthy, it extends to all belonging to all religions. Their churches shall not be lived in, they shall not be destroyed and their buildings and compounds shall not be harmed in any way. Their properties shall not be appropriated. They shall not be interfered with in their religious matters. They shall not be harmed in any other way. All that is mentioned in this deed is guaranteed by Allah, His Prophet[sa], the Khulafā and by the Muslims, the only condition being that they continue to pay the fixed amount of

Jizyah regularly."[57]

Similarly Ḥaḍrat 'Umar[ra] had issued this standing order to the officials for vigilance and not to let any Muslim be unjust to the *Dhimmī* citizens and to be vigilant against any attempt to harm their interests and to safeguard their properties against any trespass on the part of the Muslims and to see that each clause of the treaty is scrupulously honoured in every detail.[58]

Similarly the treaty with the people of ماه دینار (Māh Dīnār) also provided:

> "No attempt shall be made to force them to change their religion. Nor shall any interference be tolerated in the performance of their religious rites."[59]

In short, every single treaty that has been handed down to us through authoritative historical records provides for the full protection of the life, property and religion of the non-Muslim citizens. Their culture and civilization has invariably been left untouched and no restriction has ever been placed on their social and national life. Similarly they were excused from compulsory military service unlike the Muslims. That is why, at times, they were not allowed to wear military uniforms or to carry arms. In this connection Imam Abū Yūsuf says:

> "The non-Muslim citizens can wear any dress

> except military uniform nor can they carry arms. Because military uniform will confuse them with the Muslim soldiers."[60]

Another reason against this sartorial uniformity was that Ḥaḍrat ‘Umar[ra] insisted that the Muslims lead plain lives, wear rough home-spun stuff, and live hard and austere lives and not be self-indulgent and easy-going like the conquered Iranian.

Abū ‘Uthmān Nahdi says:

> "We were stationed in Azerbaijan under ‘Utbah bin Farqad in connection with a border expedition, "We received a directive from Ḥaḍrat ‘Umar[ra] in which he had ordered, "Wear Tehband and sheets and use sandals. Stop using trousers and socks. In short, stick to the dress of your father Ishmael. Avoid Iranian ways of living, because they would make you easy-going and self-indulgent. Live under the open skies and the sun, because they are a bath for Arabs and eliminate toxic poisons from the blood that cause disease. Lead a rigorous and exaction life".[61]

It is clear that this was a general directive which sought to inculcate in the Muslims the spirit of plain and hard living. The Muslims were, therefore, expected to wear dress which was much simpler and different from the dress the *Dhimmī* citizens were allowed to wear who were under no such obligation. Unfortunately this gave rise to confusion and misled some to believe as if a special dress had been prescribed for the *Dhimmī* citizens. All this proves that the *Dhimmī* citizens were at full liberty to wear any dress they liked and that no religious or social taboo was placed on its use. True, long after the pious Khilāfat certain restrictions were placed in the days of the Umayyads and that too under the stress of political expediency. It is a pity that the later jurists gave them a religious bias. 'Allāmah Kāshānī says:

> "The restrictions on the *Dhimmīs* were first imposed when the Umayyad Caliph 'Umar bin 'Abdul-'Azīz passed by certain riders who looked like Muslims. The caliph greeted them as such. Some of his retinue told him that they were Christians and not Muslims. He did not like this error and on return home ordered that the Christians wear Zunnar as a mark of distinction and use only a special type of saddle and not ride horses. No Muslim at the time took objection to this declaration which in time came to assume the status of Ijmā'".[62]

This extract constitutes an external evidence of the fact that right up to the days of 'Umar bin 'Abdul-'Azīz there did not exist any distinction between the Muslims and the *Dhimmīs*, and that the orders for the imposition of these restrictions were passed not by Ḥaḍrat ‘Umar[ra] but by ‘Umar bin ‘Abdul-‘Azīz, the Umayyad caliph.

Let us now take up the practice of Ḥaḍrat ‘Uthmān[ra]—the third Khalīfah and other companions of the Holy Prophet[sa]. Here, too, we do not find any social levels and distinctions between the Muslims and non-Muslims. Ḥaḍrat ‘Uthmān[ra] himself had a Christian wife named Nā’ilah, daughter of Farāfiṣah Kalbiyah. Similarly Ḥaḍrat Ṭalḥah[ra], a famous companion of the Holy Prophet[sa] had married a Syrian Jewess.[63] The same is true about the days of the fourth Khalīfah, Ḥaḍrat ‘Alī[ra], and even long after him.

Ḥaḍrat Ṣafiyyah, the mother of the faithful and wife of the Holy Prophet[sa], retained her relationships and contacts with her Jew relatives even after becoming a Muslim and marrying the Holy Prophet[sa]. Even during the days of the Holy Prophet[sa] her non-Muslim relatives were received as honoured visitors in the house of the Holy Prophet[sa]. Actually she left one third of her legacy to her nephew under her will. The nephew was a Jew.[64]

Some critics point out that doubtlessly the Muslims did have treaties with the conquered non-Muslims which were liberal and gave the *Dhimmīs* an equal status with the Muslims, but they did not honour them and live up to their spirit. They back up this objection by referring to the abrogation of treaty rights of the Jews and the Christians of Medina, Khaiber and Najrān. They were exiled and their security withdrawn. The answer to this objection is that every treaty implies certain duties which either side must carry out. Unless these duties are solemnly honoured the treaty becomes null and void. The real question is which party was guilty of violating the treaty obligations? The Jews of Medina had made this covenant with the Muslim that they would live as loyal and peaceful citizens of Muslim state, will have no truck with its enemies and will not conspire against it. The way the Jews dishonoured the solemn pledge is a matter of history. One of the clauses of the treaty was that in the event of clash with the enemy the Medinite Jews will help the Muslims. But in the Battle of Badr the Jews actively conspired against the Muslims, spied against them and altogether played a role which was against the spirit and letter of the treaty. They even went to the length of conspiring to assassinate the Holy Prophet[sa]. While the Prophet[sa] was visiting the Jewish tribe of Banū Naḍīr of Medina one of them threw a millstone on the Prophet[sa], luckily he escaped injury because of timely warning. In the Battle of Ditch, Banū Quraiẓah, another Jewish tribe of Medina, tried to stab the Muslims in the back by helping the invading Meccan army. When the Holy Prophet[sa] invoked the treaty and appealed to them to honour their obligations under the treaty, at such a crucial moment, they disowned any connection with it and declared that they did not believe in any agreements nor for that matter in any friendship with the Muslims. Actually the battle of Aḥzāb was the direct result of Jewish designs and machinations. The Jews sent out their agents to all corners of the country to fan the flames of hatred against the Muslims and to organise the Arab tribes into a united anti-Muslim front.

When the Prophet[sa] conquered Khaiber the Jews requested that they might be allowed to stay on. The Prophet[sa] accepted their request and declared:

اَقِرُّكُمْ مَا اَقَرَّكُمُ اللّٰهُ

That they could stay on as long as they maintain peace and were loyal to the state. The Jews, however, could not stay but continued to indulge in their habitual pastime of conspiring against the Muslims. They once even had the daring to throw down Ḥaḍrat 'Abdullāh bin 'Umar[ra] from the roof of a house. He did not die but sustained serious injuries.

The Christians of Najrān made secret piles of weapons of war in clear contravention of the covenant, tried to rise in revolt and establish a buffer state between Hejaz and Ethiopia. The Muslims were fighting a two-front battle against powerful foes, the forty thousand hostile Christians behind the Muslim lines were no weak threat to their security.

Under the circumstances no action which was taken against the Jews and Christians, could by any stretch of imagination, be called unjust. Particularly when it was taken to maintain law and order which is the primary duty of every government and had no bearing on the religious beliefs of the culprit. No government worth the name can permit open challenge and conspiracies under its jurisdiction. The surprising fact is that the action taken against these conspiring Jews and Christians was too mild. On their expulsion from Medina, Banū Naḍīr were permitted to remove their possessions including weapons of war. The lands of the Jews of Khaiber were purchased at the existing market rates and they were supplied with means of transport and conveyance. When the Christians of Najrān were exiled, all expenditure incurred on their movement was borne by the state. The government had issued orders that the local authorities provide them with all amenities at every halt all along the route. They were even permitted to settle in any part of Iraq or Syria and were given free lands. Further, they were given a full two years' tax holiday.[65]

In short all agreements and treaties which the Muslims made, the Islamic law pertaining to government and the way these treaties and principles were respected, as also the personal example, of the Holy Prophet[sa] himself and of his companions and Khulafā conclusively prove that the non-Muslims received the kind of sympathetic and considerate treatment at the hands of the Muslims which has no parallel in the annals of Jewish or Christian religion or of any other religion and still stands unsurpassed. It is an abject lesson to every modern secular state which faces the problem of minorities under its jurisdiction. Needless to say, that the way the Hindu India is trying to solve the problem of its Muslim minority by its liquidation and the American Whites are trying to carry the burden of the Black Negro and the Communists are handling the non-Communists has no comparison even with the treatment meted out to the minorities under some of the latter day Muslim kings whom the non-Muslim critics take pleasure in denouncing and criticizing and whose actions, it is admitted, were determined more by expediency than by their respect to Islamic law.

Right of Freedom of Expression in Islam:

Let us now take up the question of the basic human right of freedom of expression. Or, in other words let us try to determine if Islam permits non-Muslims to preach and convey the message of their religion. Technically, the Holy Quran calls it *Tablīgh*[i], which means, to state the good points of one's own religion in a positive and non-violent manner. The idea is that people become converted out of their own free choice. Objections, if any, raised against religion or its principles have to be answered rationally and calmly without breeding religious hysteria of fanatic apposition. *Tablīgh* in fact promotes the feelings of mutual trust and good-fellowship and bridges the gulf of ignorance and distrust. God says in this connection:

وَ مَنْ اَحْسَنُ قَوْلًا مِّمَّنْ دَعَآ اِلَى اللّٰهِ وَ عَمِلَ صَالِحًا وَّ قَالَ اِنَّنِيْ مِنَ
الْمُسْلِمِيْنَ ○ وَ لَا تَسْتَوِى الْحَسَنَةُ وَ لَا السَّيِّئَةُ ط اِدْفَعْ بِالَّتِيْ هِيَ
اَحْسَنُ فَاِذَا الَّذِيْ بَيْنَكَ وَ بَيْنَهٗ عَدَاوَةٌ كَاَنَّهٗ وَلِيٌّ حَمِيْمٌ ○ وَ مَا يُلَقّٰهَآ
اِلَّا الَّذِيْنَ صَبَرُوْا ج وَ مَا يُلَقّٰهَآ اِلَّا ذُوْ حَظٍّ عَظِيْمٍ ○ وَ اِمَّا يَنْزَغَنَّكَ
مِنَ الشَّيْطٰنِ نَزْغٌ فَاسْتَعِذْ بِاللّٰهِ ط اِنَّهٗ هُوَ السَّمِيْعُ الْعَلِيْمُ ○

"And Who is better in speech than he who invites *men* to Allah and does good works and says, 'I am surely of those who submit'? And good and evil are not alike. Repel *evil* with that which is best. And lo, he between whom and

---

[i] Propagating the message of one's religion.

thyself was enmity will become as though he were a warm friend. But none is granted it save those who are steadfast; and none is granted it save those who possess a large share of good. And if an incitement from Satan incite thee, then seek refuge in Allah. Surely He is the All-Hearing, the All-Knowing". (41:34-37)

Elsewhere God says:

أُدْعُ إِلَى سَبِيلِ رَبِّكَ بِالْحِكْمَةِ وَ الْمَوْعِظَةِ الْحَسَنَةِ وَ جَادِلْهُمْ بِالَّتِي
هِيَ أَحْسَنُ ؕ إِنَّ رَبَّكَ هُوَ أَعْلَمُ بِمَنْ ضَلَّ عَنْ سَبِيلِهِ وَ هُوَ أَعْلَمُ
بِالْمُهْتَدِينَ ○ وَ إِنْ عَاقَبْتُمْ فَعَاقِبُوا بِمِثْلِ مَا عُوقِبْتُمْ بِهِ ؕ وَ لَئِنْ
صَبَرْتُمْ لَهُوَ خَيْرٌ لِّلصّٰبِرِيْنَ ○

"Call unto the way of thy Lord with wisdom and goodly exhortation, and argue with them in a way that is best. Surely, they Lord knows best who has strayed away from His way; and He knows those who are rightly guided. And if you *desire to* punish *the oppressors*, then punish *them* to the extent to which you have been wronged; but if you show patience, then, surely, that is best for those who are patient. (16:126-127).

The Founder of the Ahmadiyya Movement in Islam (1835-1908), the voice-articulate of the age was especially commissioned by Allah to disseminate the message of Islam and establish its claim to be the only religion which, under the divine scheme of things, can cure human ills and solve human problems. He set up a vast missionary organization to propagate Islam. He formulated the following fundamental principles of *Tablīgh* in the light of the Holy Quran:

1. It should be accepted as a matter of principle that at the time of their inception all ancient religions were true and divine in origin. God sent Prophets and warners to every people. The fact that they have been held in high esteem, for such a long time, proves that they were no imposters.

2. Each exponent of religion should confine himself to and rely only on the text of the religious scriptures which according to his religion was revealed by God; should only refer to that book and to none other and should not extend the sphere of his exposition to give the impression as if he was engaged in inventing a new book, nor should he misappropriate the religious principles and views of other religions as his own.[66]

3. Every advocate should state the beauties of his own religion instead of attacking the other party. Because proving that other religion is wrong does not mean that his own religion is right.[67]

4. Scrupulous regard must be paid to the fact that all standards of religious controversies and discus-

sions are conducted in a decent and polite manner. Objections, if any, must be based on the standard and recognized books of the other party and not on hearsay and from which one's own religion and standard books are immune.[68]

The attention should also be invited to the purpose of religion, its life-giving influence, and the resultant love of Allah and the heavenly signs which accrue therefrom, they should also be exhorted to rely more on prayer because like physical light the true light of guidance also descends from heaven. Human conjecture and surmise cannot lead to true apprehension of God. A silent God is no God. The Perfect and Living God is One who Himself gives proof of His existence and leads us to the living religion, provided we have the craving to find the right path and have the eyes to see divine light. Therefore, the true and Living religion is one that brings man nearer to God, makes him His mouthpiece and transforms his heart into a seat of His Lord.[69]

It would not be out of place to mention a few instances of the practical application of the principles of *Tablīgh* mentioned above.

It is reported that a non-Muslim chieftain Thamāmah bin Athāl of the tribe of Yamāmah whose hostility against Muslims was well-known was arrested after a battle and was produced before the Holy Prophet[sa].

He ordered him to be confined to the Mosque. Every day the Holy Prophet[sa] would inquire how he was doing and if there was anything he wanted. Thamāmah would reply:

> "I am doing fine. If you pardon me I will remember it all my life and you will not find me ungrateful. If I am sentenced to death I deserve it. If you want ransom I will pay".

For three days Thamāmah stayed in the mosque and every day the same question and answer were repeated. Finally he was ordered to be released and allowed to go home. On release he went to a pond and had his bath and soon returned and reported to the Prophet[sa] and declared:

> "Holy Prophet[sa]! God is my witness that, on the face of the earth I hated you most, now none is dearer than you. God knows that your faith was most hateful to me but today no religion is dearer. By God, I disliked your city most but today I like it most of all the cities of the world. I accept Islam and bear witness, "there is no God but Allah and Muhammad is His exalted servant and Prophet".

Later Thamāmah visited Mecca for *'Umrah*, The Meccans threatened him because he had turned faithless. He replied:

> "I have not turned faithless but faithful because I

have accepted the best faith, the faith of Muhammad[sa]. Remember if you do not stop being hard on me you will not get a single grain of wheat from Yamāmah which is your only source of supply". The Meccans were afraid but did not care. When Thamāmah went back to Yamāmah; he appealed to his people not to sell grains to the Meccans. This restriction reduced the Meccans to serious straits of famine. At this they appealed to the Prophet[sa] begging him to interfere in the matter saying. "Our elders died in the battlefield and we ourselves are starving to death". The Prophet[sa] at once directed Thamāmah not to withhold supply of grain and to resume former commercial relations with the Meccans because, he said "to starve the enemy is wrong".[70]

Ṣafwān, son of Umayyah, was a very influential chief among the Quraish. He was a great enemy of Islam and had done all he could to destroy the Muslims. When the Holy Prophet[sa] conquered Mecca, he took refuge in Jeddah, fearing revenge from the Muslims. When the Holy Prophet[sa] came to know of his flight, he sent 'Umair[ra] to bring him back to Mecca, promising pardon for him. He came back to live in Mecca but refused to accept Islam. At the occasion of the Battle of Ḥunain, the Muslim army needed some weapons, which Ṣafwān had. The Holy

Prophet[sa] asked him to give those weapons to the Muslim army. He refused to give anything saying: 'You want to confiscate these weapons or only to borrow them?' The Holy Prophet[sa] replied: 'We only want to borrow them from you and we shall be responsible for their return'. Ṣafwān was so impressed by this that he not only gave those weapons but also joined the fold of Islam.[71]

When on the day of the conquest of Mecca, Abū Sufyān, the Chief of Mecca and an arch enemy of Islam was brought before the Holy Prophet[sa], He asked him: "Has it not dawned upon you that there is none worthy of worship except Allah". He said:

> "My father and my mother be a sacrifice to you. You have ever been kind, gentle and considerate to your relatives. I am certain that if there were anyone else worthy of worship, we might have had some help from him".
>
> The Prophet[sa] asked Him: "Has it also not dawned upon you that I am a messenger of Allah".

He replied:

> "My father and my mother be a sacrifice to you, on this I still have some doubts".

Even then the Holy Prophet[sa], forgave him. Later after the Fall of Mecca, Abū Sufyān accepted Islam.[72]

The Holy Prophet[sa] had a servant who was a Jew. Once he fell ill. When the Holy Prophet[sa] came to know of his illness, he visited him. His father was also with him. After enquiring about his health the Holy Prophet[sa] preached Islam to him. The servant looked towards his father as if asking permission from him. At this his father giving permission said: 'Accept what Muhammad says'. So he accepted Islam and recited the *Kalimah*[i]. The Holy Prophet[sa] exclaimed in delight: 'Praise be to Allah Who saved him from the Fire'.[73]

Once coming back from an expedition the Holy Prophet[sa], ordered the army to halt for a brief rest. Tired after the fight and the long journey, the Muslims lay down for rest wherever they found any shade from the sun. The Holy Prophet[sa] also found a tree, hung his sword with the tree and went to sleep. An idolater, an enemy of the Prophet[sa] was following the Muslims seeking such an opportunity. Taking the sword in his hand, he awoke the Holy Prophet[sa] and asked him mockingly: 'Muhammad now who can save you from me'? The Holy Prophet[sa] calmly replied, "Allah". Overwhelmed with the calm manner of the Holy Prophet[sa] the enemy started trembling and

---

[i] Profession of لَآاِلٰـهَ اِلَّا اللّٰهُ مُحَمَّدٌ رَّسُوْلُ اللّٰهِ i.e. There is none worthy of worship except Allah and Muhammad is His Messenger.

the sword dropped to the ground. The Holy Prophet[sa] stood up and took the sword in hand and said to him: 'Now you tell me, Who can save you from me?' The disbeliever was so astonished and overwhelmed that he was unable to reply. Hesitatingly he stammered: 'only you can, have mercy on me'. The Holy Prophet[sa], said: 'oh man! You have not learned the lesson yet, You could have said, 'Allah'. Now go freely, I do not take revenge'. The disbeliever was so impressed by the incident that he joined the fold of Islam.[74]

'Imrān, son of Ḥuṣain[ra] narrates 'Once we went on an expedition in the company of the Holy Prophet[sa]. We had no water with us and the people were thirsty. Alighting from his mount, the Holy Prophet[sa] ordered 'Alī and one other person to go in search of water. They searched for a long time but were unable to find any water. Meanwhile they saw a woman coming on a camel with two water-skins full of water. They asked her where they could find water. The woman replied: 'The water is so far from here that it is twenty-four hours since I started from there. My people are still coming behind". They said to her; 'Come with us'. She asked 'Where to'. They said 'in the presence of the Holy Prophet[sa]. She said: 'He who has turned faithless?'. They said: 'Yes, to him whom you call faithless': Thus they brought her before the

Holy Prophet[sa] and told him the conversation. The woman was asked to dismount. A big urn was placed and the water skins were opened in it. People came and took water according to their needs. Many hundreds of people quenched their thirst with it. One man wanted to have a bath. He also took water. The woman stood wondering at the strange scene. The narrator says: 'By Allah, when people stopped taking water the skins were as full as before. The Holy Prophet[sa], then asked the people to collect something to give to the woman. People collected dates, flour and *sattū*[i] and gave them to the woman. When she mounted the camel and was about to go, the Holy Prophet[sa] addressed her, 'You know, we have not taken any of your water. This was only an apparent means otherwise we were given water by Allah Himself. The woman went back to her tribe. Her people asked her where she had been. She told them the whole incident and said: 'By God either he is the greatest magician on the face of the earth or he is truly a Prophet of God'.

After this incident, although the Muslims were always engaged in fighting with the disbelievers in the vicinity but they never once interfered with her tribe. At last the woman said to her people: "Look at

---

[i] Grain parched and coarsely ground and drunk with water and sugar.

the Muslims, they have subjugated all the neighbouring tribes but have left us free only because once they took water from me. It would be, in my opinion unfortunate for us not to join such people'. The people agreed with her and the whole tribe accepted Islam.[75]

Such was the practical application of the verse:

أُدْعُ إِلَىٰ سَبِيلِ رَبِّكَ بِالْحِكْمَةِ وَالْمَوْعِظَةِ الْحَسَنَةِ

And who can object to such a manner of preaching!

Islam Guarantees Freedom of Expression:

Although, it is admitted, that there are certain Ulema who believe that Islam neither permits the non-Muslims to preach nor allows its adherents to change their faith but in reality, this belief of these Ulema is baseless and is in complete contradiction of the Islamic teachings. In the Holy Quran Allah has repeatedly asked the disbelievers to bring forth arguments in support of their claims; thus He says:

قُلْ هَلْ عِنْدَكُمْ مِّنْ عِلْمٍ فَتُخْرِجُوْهُ لَنَا ۭ اِنْ تَتَّبِعُوْنَ اِلَّا الظَّنَّ وَاِنْ اَنْتُمْ اِلَّا تَخْرُصُوْنَ

"Say, 'Have you any knowledge? Then produce it for us. You follow nothing but *mere* conjecture. And you do nothing but lie". (6:149)

Elsewhere He says:

نَبِّـُٔوۡنِیۡ بِعِلۡمٍ اِنۡ کُنۡتُمۡ صٰدِقِیۡنَ ۙ

"Inform me with knowledge, if you are truthful". (6:144)

It is clear, that if Islam were against granting the non-Muslims the rights to preach their religion, how could the Holy Quran had invited them to put forth their arguments.

Again Allah says:

وَاِنۡ کُنۡتُمۡ فِیۡ رَیۡبٍ مِّمَّا نَزَّلۡنَا عَلٰی عَبۡدِنَا فَاۡتُوۡا بِسُوۡرَۃٍ مِّنۡ مِّثۡلِہٖ ۪ وَ ادۡعُوۡا شُہَدَآءَکُمۡ مِّنۡ دُوۡنِ اللّٰہِ اِنۡ کُنۡتُمۡ صٰدِقِیۡنَ ۝

"And if you are in doubt as to what We have sent down to Our servant, then produce a Chapter like it, and call upon your helpers beside Allah, if you are truthful". (2:24)

Again He says:

قُلۡ اِنَّمَاۤ اَعِظُکُمۡ بِوَاحِدَۃٍ ۚ اَنۡ تَقُوۡمُوۡا لِلّٰہِ مَثۡنٰی وَ فُرَادٰی ثُمَّ تَتَفَکَّرُوۡا ۟ مَا بِصَاحِبِکُمۡ مِّنۡ جِنَّۃٍ ؕ اِنۡ ہُوَ اِلَّا نَذِیۡرٌ لَّکُمۡ بَیۡنَ یَدَیۡ عَذَابٍ شَدِیۡدٍ ۝ قُلۡ مَا سَاَلۡتُکُمۡ مِّنۡ اَجۡرٍ فَہُوَ لَکُمۡ ؕ اِنۡ اَجۡرِیَ اِلَّا عَلَی اللّٰہِ ۚ وَ ہُوَ عَلٰی کُلِّ شَیۡءٍ شَہِیۡدٌ ۝ ... قُلۡ اِنۡ ضَلَلۡتُ

فَاِنَّمَآ اَضِلُّ عَلٰى نَفْسِيْ ۚ وَ اِنِ اهْتَدَيْتُ فَبِمَا يُوْحِيْٓ اِلَيَّ رَبِّيْ ۭ اِنَّهٗ
سَمِيْعٌ قَرِيْبٌ ۝

"Say, 'I only exhort you *to do* one thing: that you stand up before Allah in twos and singly and then reflect. *You will then know that* there is no insanity in your companion; he is only a Warner to you of an impending severe punishment'. Say, 'Whatever reward I might have asked of you—let it be yours. My reward is only with Allah; And He is Witness over all things'.... Say, 'If I err, I err only against myself; and if I am rightly guided, it is because of what my Lord has revealed to me. Verily, He is All-Hearing, Nigh". (34:47, 48, 51)

It is clear from the above-quoted verses of the Holy Quran that to compel anyone to forsake his faith is something very unreasonable and futile. And even if it were allowed to compel anyone in religious matters, then God Himself was enough to compel. He was not in need of any help for this. He Himself says:

وَ لَوْ شَآءَ رَبُّكَ لَاٰمَنَ مَنْ فِي الْاَرْضِ كُلُّهُمْ جَمِيْعًا ۭ اَفَاَنْتَ تُكْرِهُ
النَّاسَ حَتّٰى يَكُوْنُوْا مُؤْمِنِيْنَ ۝

"And if thy Lord had *enforced* His will, surely, all who are on the earth would have believed together. Wilt thou, then, force men to become believers'. (10:100).

Thus when God Himself has left the matter of religion to the man, who else has the right to compel anyone? In short, neither does Islam encourage its adherents to compel the disbelievers to join Islam nor does it tolerate others to compel the Muslims to turn faithless. The call to faith, according to Islam, should be based on sincerity and human sympathy. Therefore it is, that in the face of opposition, the Prophets of Allah have always said:

أُبَلِّغُكُمْ رِسٰلٰتِ رَبِّيْ وَأَنَا لَكُمْ نَاصِحٌ أَمِيْنٌ ○

"I deliver to you the messages of my Lord and I am to you a sincere and faithful counsellor". (7:69)

Elsewhere the Holy Quran pointing out the two primary duties of God's messengers says:

رُسُلًا مُّبَشِّرِيْنَ وَ مُنْذِرِيْنَ لِئَلَّا يَكُوْنَ لِلنَّاسِ عَلَى اللّٰهِ حُجَّةٌ بَعْدَ الرُّسُلِ ؕ وَ كَانَ اللّٰهُ عَزِيْزًا حَكِيْمًا ○

"Messengers, bearers of glad tidings and warners, so that people may have no plea against Allah after *the coming of* the Messengers. And Allah is Mighty, Wise". (4:166)

The meanings of this verse are quite clear. If the disbelievers are not even permitted to put forth their own arguments in support of their faith then what is the significance of the words *So that people may have no plea against Allah*.

Elsewhere the Holy Quran speaks of the wrath of God against those who use force to stop others to preach their religion. It says:

وَاضْرِبْ لَهُمْ مَّثَلًا اَصْحٰبَ الْقَرْيَةِ ۘ اِذْ جَآءَهَا الْمُرْسَلُوْنَ ۝ اِذْ
اَرْسَلْنَآ اِلَيْهِمُ اثْنَيْنِ فَكَذَّبُوْهُمَا فَعَزَّزْنَا بِثَالِثٍ فَقَالُوْٓا اِنَّآ اِلَيْكُمْ
مُّرْسَلُوْنَ ۝ قَالُوْا مَآ اَنْتُمْ اِلَّا بَشَرٌ مِّثْلُنَا ۙ وَمَآ اَنْزَلَ الرَّحْمٰنُ مِنْ
شَیْءٍ ۙ اِنْ اَنْتُمْ اِلَّا تَكْذِبُوْنَ ۝ قَالُوْا رَبُّنَا يَعْلَمُ اِنَّآ اِلَيْكُمْ
لَمُرْسَلُوْنَ ۝ وَمَا عَلَيْنَآ اِلَّا الْبَلٰغُ الْمُبِيْنُ ۝ قَالُوْٓا اِنَّا تَطَيَّرْنَا بِكُمْ ۚ
لَئِنْ لَّمْ تَنْتَهُوْا لَنَرْجُمَنَّكُمْ وَلَيَمَسَّنَّكُمْ مِّنَّا عَذَابٌ اَلِيْمٌ ۝ قَالُوْا
طَآئِرُكُمْ مَّعَكُمْ ۭ اَئِنْ ذُكِّرْتُمْ ۭ بَلْ اَنْتُمْ قَوْمٌ مُّسْرِفُوْنَ ۝

"And set forth to them the parable of a people of the town, when the Messengers came to it. When We sent to them two Messengers and they rejected them both; so we strengthened *them* by a third, and they said, 'verily we have been sent to you as Messengers'. They replied, 'You are but men like us and the Gracious *God* has not revealed anything. You only lie. 'They said, 'Our Lord knows that we are indeed His Messengers to you; And on us lies only the plain delivery of the Message'. They said, 'Surely we augur evil

> fortune from you; if you desist not, we will certainly stone you, and a painful punishment will surely befall you at our hands'. They replied, 'Your evil fortune is with your own selves. Is it because you have been admonished? Nay, you are a people transgressing all bounds".(36:14-20)

All these verses and the examples from the life of the Holy Prophet[sa] related in the foregoing pages, clearly prove that contrary to the beliefs of certain so-called Muslim Ulema and critics of Islam, it not only grants to the non-Muslims the freedom to preach and convey the message of their faith but also encourages the holding of religious dialogues between the adherents of different religions. The only restriction imposed by Islam is that such debates should be held in an atmosphere of good-fellowship and should be conducted in a positive and constructive manner.

The fact of the matter is that only that religious community fears to allow other peoples to preach their faith which, either realizing the weaknesses and unreasonableness of its own religion tacitly acknowledges the superiority of other faiths, or whose elders, ignoring their duty to teach their people in the fundamentals of their faith, leave them ignorant of their own religion, so that when attacked by others, knowing nothing about their own beliefs, they have to remain silent. Because any religion, which has reasonable and irrefutable arguments behind it and which can satisfy the questions of the human mind, has nothing to fear from allowing other religions to preach. Similarly any community whose people are educated in the fundamentals of their faith and are satisfied with what they believe in, has nothing to be afraid of.

A man changes his faith only when he feels dissatisfied with his own faith. And when he thinks he can find satisfaction in a new faith he joins it. If there is any faith which satisfies the questioning mind of a man and removes all his doubts and answers all the cravings of his nature, its adherents will never think of changing their faith, even if all the preachers in the world were to preach to them. On the other hand, if any people are dissatisfied with their beliefs, no measure of force could make them stick to their own beliefs. Because although, by the use of force, the people can be compelled to conform to the outward observance of their faith but in their hearts they would no longer belong to that religion.

Further, any restriction on free exchange of views will cause a mental inertia in a people. The confrontation of different civilizations and the free exchange of views among the followers of different ideologies is the main source of development of knowledge.

Without the free exchange of views, the human mind will become like stagnant water and will lose all its freshness. And this will undoubtedly cause the downfall of any people who are stupid enough to impose such restrictions. As regards Islam, it should be noted that all the earliest wars that the Muslims fought were fought because their opponents denied them the basic human right of freedom of speech. After the advent of the Holy Prophet[sa], when he began to preach to the people of Mecca, the chiefs of Mecca tried to persuade him to keep his views with him and not to preach them. First they tried to buy his silence by offering him wealth and chiefdom of Mecca. When the Holy Prophet[sa] refused, they decided to use force in silencing him. They decided not to meet argument by argument but to draw the sword and put down the new teaching by force. The Holy Prophet[sa] and his followers suffered continuously and consistently at the hands of the Meccan disbelievers and even after they escaped to Medina to uphold their right to profess, practice and preach what they believed, they were not left alone. The ruthless Quraish attacked them time and again. The enemy was out to extirpate Islam, it was therefore necessary to fight the enemy in defence to truth and freedom of belief. Otherwise they would have been forced to surrender their conscience to the disbelievers.

How then, could it be possible for the Holy Prophet[sa] to usurp the very right to uphold which he underwent untold miseries and sufferings at the hands of his enemies. Especially since in the very early days of Islam when only a handful and weak persons had joined him Allah said to him:

فَذَكِّرْ ۟ إِنَّمَآ أَنْتَ مُذَكِّرٌ ۝ لَسْتَ عَلَيْهِمْ بِمُصَيْطِرٍ ۝

"Admonish, therefore, for thou art but an admonisher; Thou hast no authority to *compel* them". (88:22, 23)

The Prophet[sa] was told that a day would come when he would be given power and authority over all his enemies and he was enjoined in advance that when he should have power he should not use it for usurping his enemy's right to freedom of speech and should not try to impose his own opinions on them. God says:

لَآ إِكْرَاهَ فِي الدِّيْنِ ۙ قَدْ تَّبَيَّنَ الرُّشْدُ مِنَ الْغَيِّ ۚ فَمَنْ يَّكْفُرْ بِالطَّاغُوْتِ وَ يُؤْمِنْ بِاللّٰهِ فَقَدِ اسْتَمْسَكَ بِالْعُرْوَةِ الْوُثْقٰى ۙ لَا انْفِصَامَ لَهَا ۗ وَ اللّٰهُ سَمِيْعٌ عَلِيْمٌ ۝

"There should be no compulsion in religion. Surely, right has become distinct from wrong; so whosoever refuses to be led by those who transgress, and believes in Allah, has surely grasped a strong handle which knows no breaking. And Allah is All-Hearing, All Knowing".(2:257)

The verse is the clearest declaration of the fundamental human right of the freedom of religion. In the face of such a declaration it is the height of injustice to accuse Islam of countenancing the use of force in matters of religion. It not only commands the Muslims not to use force to convert the non-Muslims to Islam, but also gives reason why it should not be used, saying: 'Surely, right has become distinct from wrong', i.e. the true path has become distinct from the wrong one and anyone who desires to see this true path can easily see it, but if anyone does not desire to see it, no force can possibly make him do so'.

Faith or *Īmān* according to Islam consists in believing in a thing with the heart or mind and the expressing that belief with the tongue. The use of force can compel a man to proclaim the faith with his tongue but no measure of force can bring about a change in the heart.

Allah says:

قُلْ يَآأَيُّهَا الْكَٰفِرُونَ... لَكُمْ دِينُكُمْ وَلِيَ دِينِ ۝

O Prophet "Say: 'O Ye disbelievers!...For you your religion, and for me my religion'. (109:2, 7)

Referring to the differences among the religions God says:

لِكُلِّ اُمَّةٍ جَعَلْنَا مَنْسَكًا هُمْ نَاسِكُوْهُ فَلَا يُنَازِعُنَّكَ فِي الْاَمْرِ وَادْعُ اِلٰى رَبِّكَ ؕ اِنَّكَ لَعَلٰى هُدًى مُّسْتَقِيْمٍ ۝

"To every people have We appointed ways of worship which they observe; so let them not dispute with thee in the matter; and invite thou to thy Lord, for surely, thou followest the right guidance".(22:68)

Elsewhere He says:

لِكُلٍّ جَعَلْنَا مِنْكُمْ شِرْعَةً وَّ مِنْهَاجًا ؕ وَ لَوْ شَآءَ اللّٰهُ لَجَعَلَكُمْ اُمَّةً وَّاحِدَةً وَّ لٰكِنْ لِّيَبْلُوَكُمْ فِيْ مَآ اٰتٰـكُمْ فَاسْتَبِقُوا الْخَيْرٰتِ ؕ اِلَى اللّٰهِ مَرْجِعُكُمْ جَمِيْعًا فَيُنَبِّئُكُمْ بِمَا كُنْتُمْ فِيْهِ تَخْتَلِفُوْنَ ۝

"For each of you We prescribed a clear spiritual Law and a manifest way *in secular matters*. And if Allah had *enforced* His will, He would have made you *all* one people, but *He wishes* to try you by that which He has given you. Vie, then, with one another in good works. To Allah shall you all return; then will He inform you of that wherein you differed". (5:49)

Again addressing the Holy Prophet[sa] God says:

وَقُل لِّلَّذِينَ أُوتُوا الْكِتَٰبَ وَالْأُمِّيِّنَ ءَأَسْلَمْتُمْ ۚ فَإِنْ أَسْلَمُوا فَقَدِ
اهْتَدَوا ۖ وَّإِن تَوَلَّوْا فَإِنَّمَا عَلَيْكَ الْبَلَٰغُ ۗ

"And say to those who have been given the Book and to the unlearned, 'Have you submitted?' If they submit, then they will surely be guided; but if they turn back, then thy duty is only to convey the message". (3:21)

References

1. Ṭabaqāt Ibn-e-Sa'd, Vol. I, p. 97. (Beirut 1996)
2. Ṭabaqāt Ibn-e-Sa'd, Vol. II, p. 318; (Beirut 1996)
   Tārīkhul-Khamīs, Part II, p. 88. Bāb Dhikrul-Aṣnām Kānat fil Bait
3. Naṣbur-Rāyah li Aḥādīthul-Hadāyah, Vol. III, p. 381. (Dārul-Māmūn 1938)
4. Naṣbur-Rāyah li Aḥādīthul-Hadāyah, Vol. III, p. 381. (Dārul-Māmūn 1938)
5. Ṭabrī, Part V, pp. 27-28. (Beirut 1998)
6. Naṣbur-Rāyah li Aḥādīthul-Hadāyah, Vol. III, p. 380. (Dārul-Māmūn 1938)
7. Hidāyah Vol. II, Kitābus-Siyar, p. 562. (Cairo 2008)
8. Ṭabaqāt Ibn-e-Sa'd, Vol. I, pp. 173-174. (Beirut 1996)
   Bukhārī, Kitābul-Wakālah, Hadith 2141.
9. Sīratul-Ḥalbiyyah, Vol. III, p. 81. (Beirut 2002)
10. Musnad Aḥmad Bin Ḥanbal, Vol. IV, p. 543, Hadith 13233. (Beirut 1998)
11. Musnad Aḥmad Bin Ḥanbal Vol. VII, pp. 899-900, Hadith 24343. (Beirut 1998)
12. Tirmidhī, Abwābul-Aṭ'imah, Hadith 1819. (Beirut 2002)
13. Zādul-Ma'ād, Vol. I, pp. 141-142.
14. Abū Dāwūd, Kitābul-Khirāj, Hadith 3055. ((Riyadh 2007)
15. Aḥkāmul-Quran, Vol. III, p. 88. (Suhail Academy, Lahore)
16. Saḥīḥ Bukhārī, i.e. Tajrīd-Bukhārī, Kitābul-Jihād, Hadith 1262, pp. 530-531. (Karachi 2007)

17. Abū Dāwūd, Kitābul-Khirāj, Hadith 3050. (Riyadh 2007)
18. Abū Dāwūd, Kitābul-Jihād, Hadith 2705. (Riyadh 2007)
19. Musnad Aḥmad Bin Ḥanbal, Vol. V, pp. 584-585, Hadith 15588, 15589. (Beirut 1998)
20. Fatūhul-Buldān, p. 24. (Beirut 2000)
21. Izālatul-Khifā' 'an Khilāfatil-Khulafā', Section 2, p. 120. (Suhail Academy, Lahore 1976)
22. Fatūhul-Buldān, pp.87-88. (Beirut 2000)
Kitābul-Khirāj, p. 149. (Chapter Kanā'is wal Bai')
23. Al-Fārūq by Shiblī Nu'mānī, pp. 212-213. (Karachi 2004)
24. Saḥīḥ Bukhārī, Kitābul-Farḍul-Khumus, Hadith 3152.
Saḥīḥ Bukhārī, Kitābul-Jizyah wal-Muwādi'ah, Hadith 3162.
Aḥkāmus-Sulṭāniyyah, p. 153. (Waḍ'il-Khirāj wl-Jizyah)
25. Kitābul-Khirāj, pp. 155-156. (Chapter Kanā'is wal Bai')
26. Kitābul-Amwāl, Abū 'Ubaid Qāsim bin Salām.
27. Izālatul-Khifā' 'an Khilāfatil-Khulafā', Part II, p. 73. (Suhail Academy, Lahore 1976)
Kitābul-Khirāj, p. 136. (Chapter man Tujib 'alaihil-Jizyah)
Fatūhul-Buldān, p. 136. (Beirut 2000)
Kanzul-'Ummāl. Part III, Kitābul-Jihād, p. 213, Hadith 11473. (Beirut 2004)
28. Kitābul-Khirāj, pp. 118-119. (Chapter Taqbīlis-Sawād)
29. Moqraisy, Vol.1, p.74. as quoted by Shiblī in Al-Fārūq part 2, p. 183. (Kānpūr 1899).
30. Memory of Fatūhush-Shām, p.106.
31. Ahde-Nabwī Meiṅ Niẓām-e-Ḥukmarānī, p. 157. (Urdu Academy Sind, Karachi 1987).

32. Da'wat-e-Islām, p. 263. (Lahore 2009)
33. Naṣbur-Rāyah li Aḥādīthul-Hadāyah, Vol. IV, p. 336. (Dārul-Māmūn 1938)
34. Naṣbur-Rāyah li Aḥādīthul-Hadāyah, Vol. IV, p. 337. (Dārul-Māmūn 1938)
35. Kanzul-'Ummāl Vol. XII, p. 294, Hadith 36005. (Beirut 2004)
36. Aḥkāmul-Quran Vol. II, pp. 279-280. (Suhail Academy, Lahore 1976)
37. Al-Īḍāḥ.
    Durr-e-Mukhtār Vol. I, Kitābul-Jihād, pp. 351-352. (Educational Press Karachi)
38. Aḥkāmus-Sulṭāniyyah, p. 160. (Chapter Waḍ'il Khirāj wal Jizyah)
39. Ṭabrī, Vol. V, pp. 27-28. (Beirut 1998)
40. Tārīkh-e-Tamaddunal-Islāmī, Vol. I, p. 219. (Maktabatul-Ḥayāt, Beirut)
41. A'ẓamul-Kalām, Part I, pp. 58-59. (Agrah 1910)
42. Saḥīḥ Bukhārī, Kitābul-Hajj, Hadith 1739.
43. Tajrīdul-Bukhārī, Kitābul-Jihād, p. 532, Hadith 1265. (Karachi 2007)
44. Hidāyah, Vol. II, pp. 599-600. (Cairo 2008)
45. Baḥrur-Rā'iq Sharaḥ Kanzud-Daqā'iq, Vol. V, pp. 113-114. (Maktabah Mājdiyyah Quetta)
    Kanzud-Daqā'iq, Kitābus-Siyar wal-Jihād, p. 241. (Maktabah Raḥmāniyyah Lahore)
46. Hidāyah, Vol. II, Kitābus-Siyar, p. 600. (Cairo 2008)
    Baḥrur-Rā'iq Sharaḥ Kanzud-Daqā'iq, Vol. V, p. 114.

(Maktabah Mājdiyyah Quetta)

47. Hidāyah, Vol. II, Kitābus-Siyar, p. 600. (Cairo 2008)
    Al-Ikhtiyārātul-'Ilmiyyah, Kitābul-Jihād, p. 189. (Kirghistānul-'Ilmiyyah 1329 AH)
    Kanzud-Daqā'iq, Kitābus-Siyar wal-Jihād, p. 241. (Maktabah Raḥmāniyyah Lahore)
    Baḥrur-Rā'iq Sharaḥ Kanzud-Daqā'iq, Vol. V, p. 114. (Maktabah Mājdiyyah Quetta)
    Tabyīnul-Haqā'iq, Vol. III, Kitābus-Siyar, p. 281. (Cairo 1313 AH)
48. Hidāyah Vol. II, Kitābus-Siyar, p. 599. (Cairo 2008)
    Badāi'uṣ-Ṣanā'i', Vol. VII, Kitābus-Siyar, p. 113. (Maktabah Rashīd Quetta 1990)
    Baḥrur-Rā'iq Sharaḥ Kanzud-Daqā'iq, Vol. V, p. 112. (Maktabah Mājdiyyah Quetta)
    Baḥrur-Rā'iq Sharaḥ Kanzud-Daqā'iq, Vol. VII, p. 214. (Maktabah Mājdiyyah Quetta)
49. Baḥrur-Rā'iq Vol.V, p. 112. (Maktabah Mājdiyyah Quetta)
50. Hidāyah Vol. II, Kitābus-Siyar, p. 600. (Cairo 2008)
    Baḥrur-Rā'iq Sharaḥ Kanzud-Daqā'iq, Vol. V, p. 113. (Maktabah Mājdiyyah Quetta)
    Badāi'uṣ-Ṣanā'i', Vol. VII, Kitābus-Siyar, p. 113. (Maktabah Rashīd Quetta 1990)
51. Tārīkh-e-Tamaddunal-Islāmī Vol. III, p. 180. (Maktabatul-Ḥayāt, Beirut)
52. Al-Hārūn, p. 284.
53. The History of Spain by Louis Bertrand, Part I, p. 32.

54. Kanzud-Daqā'iq, Kitābus-Siyar wal-Jihād, p. 241. (Maktabah Raḥmāniyyah Lahore)
55. Gharā'ibush-Shu'bah, narrated by Ibn-e-Mandah.
Kanzul-'Ummāl. Part III, Kitābul-Jihad, pp. 215-216. Hadith 11489. (Beirut 2004)
56. Izālatul-Khifā' 'an Khilāfatil-Khulafā', Section 2, p. 135. (Suhail Academy, Lahore 1976)
57. Ṭabrī, Vol. IV, p. 191. (Beirut 1998)
58. Kitābul-Khirāj, p. 152. (Chapter Kanā'is wal Bai')
59. Ṭabrī, Vol. V, p. 18. (Beirut 1998)
60. Kitābul-Khirāj, p. 156. (Chapter Kanā'is wal Bai')
61. Izālatul-Khifā' 'an Khilāfatil-Khulafā', Section 2, pp. 206-207. (Suhail Academy, Lahore 1976)
62. Badāi'uṣ-Ṣanā'i', Vol. VII, Kitābus-Siyar, p. 113. (Maktabah Rashīd Quetta 1990)
63. Aḥkāmul-Quran, Vol. II, p. 325. (Suhail Academy, Lahore 1976)
64. Sharaḥ Zurqānī. Vol. IV, p. 436. Chapter Fī Azwājihī... Ṣafiyyah (Beirut 1996)
65. Fatūḥul-Buldān, p. 47. (Beirut 2000)
Sīratun-Nabawiyyah by Ibn-e-Hishām, p. 48. (Beirut 2001)
Fatḥul-Bārī Vol. V, Kitābul-Ḥarth wal-Mazāri'ah, p. 14. (Qadīmī Kutub Khānah, Karachi)
Kitābul-Khirāj, pp. 79-80. (Chapter Qissah Najrān wa Ahluhā)
66. Philosophy of the Teachings of Islam, Rūḥānī Khazā'in, Vol X, p. 315.
67. Barāhīn-i-Ahmadiyya, Part II, Rūḥānī Khazā'in, Vol I, pp. 89-91.

68. Tablīgh-i-Risālat Vol. VII, p. 16.
69. Philosophy of the Teachings of Islam, Rūḥānī Khazā'in, Vol X, pp. 443-444.
70. Tajrīdul-Bukhārī, Kitābul-Maghāzī, p. 650 Hadith 1575. (Dārul-Ishā'at, Karachi 2007)
    Sīratun-Nabawiyyah by Ibn-e-Hishām, p. 888. (Beirut 2001)
71. Sunan Al-Kubrā by Baihqi, Kitāb Qasmiṣ-Ṣadaqāt, Hadith 13185 (Beirut 2003)
72. Sīratun-Nabawiyyah by Ibn-e-Hishām, p. 737. (Beirut 2001)
    Ṭabaqāt Ibn-e-Sa'd Vol. II. p. 317. (Beirut 1996)
73. Musnad Aḥmad Bin Ḥanbal, Vol. IV, p. 451, Hadith 12823. (Beirut 1996)
74. Tajrīdul-Bukhārī, Kitābul-Maghāzī, p. 627, Hadith 1529. (Dārul-Ishā'at, Karachi 2007)
75. Tajrīdul-Bukhārī, Kitābut-Tayammum, pp. 142-143, Hadith 227. (Dārul-Ishā'at, Karachi 2007)

CPSIA information can be obtained
at www.ICGtesting.com
Printed in the USA
LVHW050759130422
716028LV00014B/733

9 781848 808492